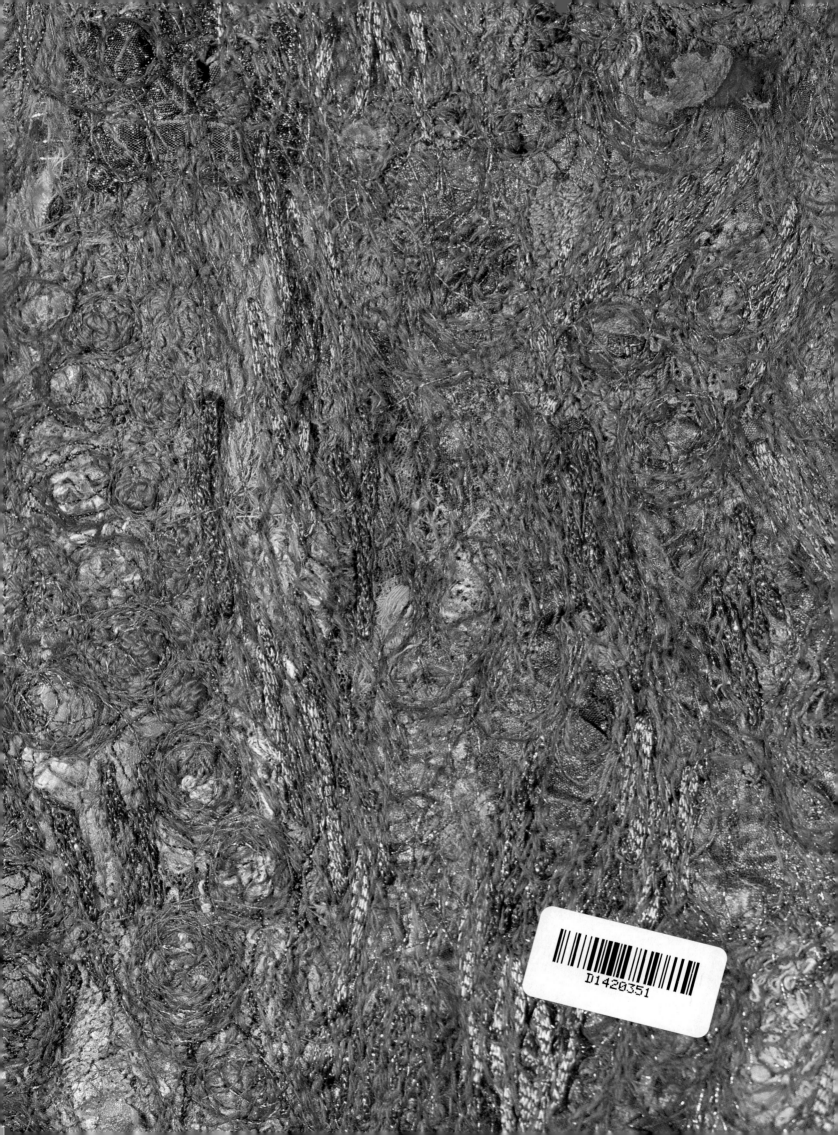

A COMPLETE GUIDE TO

CREATIVE EMBROIDERY

DESIGNS · TEXTURES · STITCHES

Jan Beaney and Jean Littlejohn

CENTURY
LONDON SYDNEY AUCKLAND JOHANNESBURG

*To Steve and Philip for their continuing support
and encouragement*

PHOTOGRAPHY BY DUDLEY MOSS

Edited by Cindy Richards
Designed by Sue Storey
Still Life Photography on pages 10, 22, 35, 46, 49 (top),
94 (bottom), 96, 121 (top), 122 and 124 by Patrick McLeavey
Location photography by Jan Beaney, Jean Littlejohn,
Philip Littlejohn, Steve Udall
Stitch Illustrations by Dennis Hawkins

First published in 1991 by Century Editions, an imprint
of the Random Century Group Ltd, 20 Vauxhall Bridge Road,
London SW1V 2SA

Random Century Australia Pty Ltd,
20 Alfred Street,
Milsons Point, Sydney, NSW 2061, Australia

Random Century New Zealand Ltd, 18 Poland Road,
Glenfield, Auckland 10, New Zealand

Random Century South Africa (Pty) Ltd, PO Box 337,
Bergvlei, 2012 South Africa

Typeset by SX Composing, Rayleigh, Essex
Printed and bound in Hong Kong

A catalogue record for this book is available
from the British Library

ISBN 0 7126 4581 0

Front cover: (clockwise from top left) Abstract Pattern by
Elizabeth Coughlan, Feathers *by Anne Jones,* Cathedral *by
Barbara Young,* Coloured Grasses *by Jan Beaney.*

Endpapers: Tree Celebration II *by Jean Littlejohn*

Opposite title page: *colourful abstract embroidery, based
on cave formations, by Diane Kelly. The pattern of vertical
stripes relates to the stalagmites and stalactites of the
original cave.*

CONTENTS

PREFACE

Embroidery can be a sharing experience and it is stimulating to exchange ideas. We have been most fortunate over a period of years not only to share a friendship and a passion for stitched textiles but also to be in a position to work as a team, bouncing ideas from one to another.

We are not always aware of who initiates the starting points but being in a position to talk and mull over these thoughts enables us to plan a structured approach to our teaching as well as being an enjoyable experience.

Within this framework we retain our individual approaches and style of working.

There are many ways of achieving a piece of creative stitching and we would not presume that the approach we offer in these books is the only way.

For many years we have encouraged students to develop their ideas beyond the superficial by extended themes and this has been reflected in the way we have planned both books.

In some instances you may find the glossary we have compiled useful (see page 138).

We believe that many people are capable of designing and stitching their own embroideries. Our students have found our methods reassuring. Our message is not to be intimidated but to enjoy learning to look and explore the creative potential of papers, fabrics and threads.

DESIGN TO EMBROIDER

Jean Littlejohn

Above: *detail of paper chickens by Phil Palmer (page 55).*

Opposite page: *geometric design and canvas-work sample by Elizabeth Coughlan.*

CONTENTS

INTRODUCTION

The ability to draw and design is within the reach of everyone but lack of confidence so often prevents people from achieving their full potential.

In many cultures, drawing skills are part of a way of life and not held up as an exclusive gift available only to those with natural ability. Just as competence in writing, mathematics or music may be improved with practice and enthusiasm, so it is with drawing.

Through drawing we learn to see. We may think we know a familiar flower until asked to describe it accurately. By recording it on paper we cannot help but understand it better.

There are very few people who can sit in front of a blank sheet of paper and conjure up designs purely from imagination. Most of us need to look at a source of inspiration and from it develop ideas which will work in fabric and thread.

To do this it is necessary to be aware of the widest possible range of media and techniques in order to select those which suit our personal style and the embroideries we plan to work.

All of the techniques in the book are based on simple principles and, most importantly, capable of being carried out at home using accessible equipment.

It has become apparent that many people would like a structured approach towards designing which will not only inspire images for embroidery, but establish confidence and act as a springboard for new and stimulating ways of working.

This book contains a range of ideas from basic backgrounds and simple mark-making through to more complex multimedia work. The ideas are there to inspire rather than follow slavishly, but the guidelines will encourage those first marks.

It is important to remember the need to experiment and not to give up if first attempts do not achieve the desired effect. Several of the designs featured in the book were done by people who started out with very little confidence in either drawing or designing, others by experienced artists. Just remember that with practice and curiosity anything is possible.

Above: *a tissue paper collage and painted pattern by Clémence Gilder.*

MARK-MAKING MATERIALS

A visit to any art shop will reveal the huge range of paints, crayons, inks, pencils, papers and glues available. These provide exciting design possibilities but hasty choices can result in costly mistakes. How do you decide which ones to buy? Many people have visually appealing boxed sets of colouring media which remain unused. Ideally it would be marvellous to be let loose in an art shop and try everything before buying, indeed some shops have samples for this purpose, so it is always worth asking. Being watched doesn't matter as simple lines and smudges will suffice to indicate if you like the feel, the mark or even the sound a material makes on the paper. Conté pencils have a wonderful colour range and blend beautifully but can make a rasping noise on textured paper which you may find unpleasant, so it is wise to try them before committing yourself to a complete box.

Before buying anything search your house, ask members of your family for contributions, and I bet you'll be amazed at the range of mark-making materials you already have. For linear marks fibre tip pens, pencils, ink pens and ballpoint pens will offer a very wide range. Alternatively, if you are part of a group, pool your resources for one session and try each other's materials. Using simple marks build up a chart making careful note of the name and type of material used next to each one with additional comments on its handling and potential – it will prove an invaluable source of reference.

Selecting your materials need not be complicated if a little common sense is applied. Look upon the various types of colouring media as pigments bound together in different ways. Being aware of the composition will indicate what it does. Perhaps the most effective method of selection would be to consider the quality of mark you are seeking and think in terms of line, tonal values, boldness, subtlety, vibrancy, delicacy, coarseness and texture.

This collection of design materials was accumulated over a period of years. Among the more sophisticated equipment there are everyday items such as sponges, drinking straws and an old toothbrush all of which can be very useful.

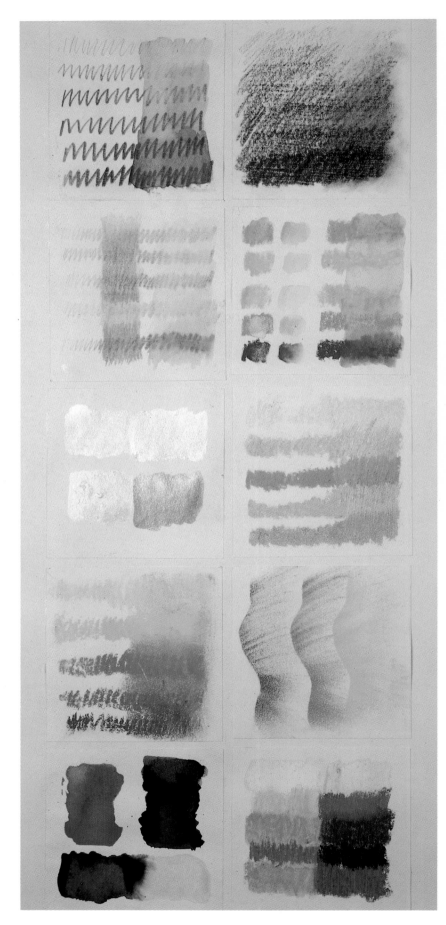

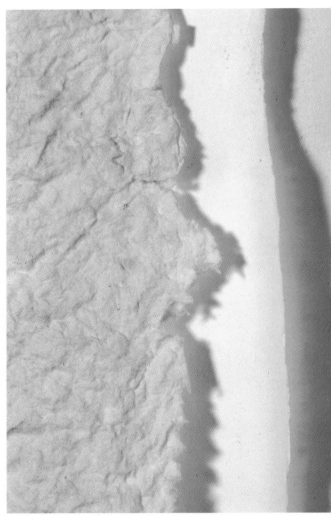

From the top: *Aquarelle drawing pencils* (left), *medium and dark, blendable with water. A 6B graphite stick* (right) *is soft and can be used to shade light and heavy tones. Fine Aquarelle pencils* (left) *are used for subtle colour blending and make a delicate wash when brushed with clean water. Aquarelle crayons and thick soft pencils* (right) *are excellent for rich spreads of colour when brushed with clean water. Palettes of dry colour can be made in a sketchbook and lifted with water to produce a colour wash which is very useful for trips and museum visits. Iridescent gouache paints* (left) *have a lustrous quality which is very useful when designing for pearlized silk paints. Pearlized oil pastels* (right) *have a soft rich texture. A degree of blending may be achieved by dragging colours together with a blunt tool or working them into each other.*

Pastels (left), *soft and chalky in texture, can be easily smudged and blended but need fixing. Rub soft chalky pastel powder* (right) *across the edge of a template to achieve subtle images. Drawing inks* (left), *available in many colours, have great vibrancy and give colourful intensity to a design. The colourful richness of oil pastels* (right) *can be useful to create textured surfaces.*

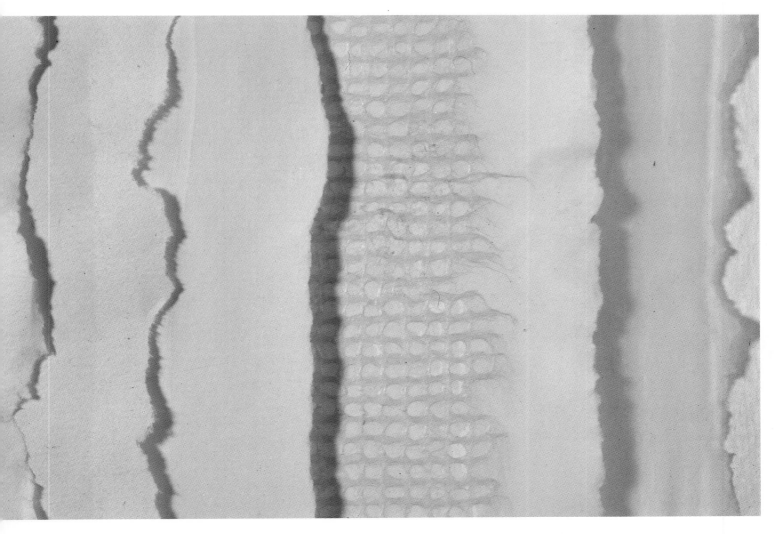

BACKGROUND PAPERS

When selecting fabrics for embroidery we are careful to find the appropriate quality and texture for the type of work. Paper, a crucial factor in any design work, is equally worthy of thought. Paper is a fibrous material composed of wood or rag pulp. It can be textured or smooth, matt or shiny, semi-transparent or thick and chunky, soft and absorbent or resistant to moisture.

So, not only do you have an enormous range of media, but types of surface on which to work them. For example, a wax crayon will glide smoothly over a card surface in contrast to the resistance encountered on a heavy watercolour paper.

As with the different media there is no better alternative than to experiment. Make a collection of every type of paper you can find, even the most mundane household papers, for example, tissue paper from shoe boxes, wallpaper scraps, kitchen towel and brown wrapping paper, will all prove useful. The occasional specialized paper such as the fine delicate semi-transparent Japanese or heavy watercolour papers are a pleasure to use. (Throughout the book any effect which is achieved on a specific background will be clearly stated.)

Handling papers will also emphasize their properties. Do they tear evenly or in a jagged way? How well can they be folded or manipulated? The quality and nature of the fibre will affect this and dictate the absorbency of the surface. Handmade paper is widely used in textile design and incorporated in embroidery. Old papers and offcuts from designing can be recycled into thick rich uneven handmade papers or delicate fibrous surfaces. If left unsealed they can be difficult to draw on and soak up ink and paint like a sponge, but there are occasions when this is right for a specific image.

Where the whiteness and glare of the paper is distracting a fine wash of tea, applied with a sponge or brush, will make a more receptive surface (see above). It should also be remembered that drawing can look good on prepared, textured or patterned, papers of which there are many examples in the following pages.

Each of the papers (above) was brushed gently with the same strength wash of tea. The various tones indicate the degree of absorbency of the different surfaces. From left to right: *handmade, ingres, blotting, recycled cartridge, Japanese, cartridge, tissue and watercolour papers. Note also the way in which they have torn, another indication of their fibre qualities.*

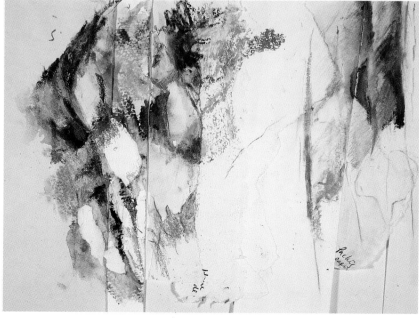

INTERPRETING AN IMAGE

Working in abstract smudges and lines is ideal when discovering the attributes of drawing media and backgrounds. The next stage is to discover what happens when you want to use the materials with control and judgement.

A collection of objects which appeal and offer varied surfaces will provide the inspiration here. For instance, pebbles, stones, fossils, plant materials and feathers will give a huge variety of textures. Man-made objects such as pieces of rust, machine parts and plastics may also prove challenging. All will provide a good opportunity to sharpen up your critical faculties. Consider which is the shiniest, the softest, or the most coarse and grainy, by handling and observation.

It is not necessary at first to draw outlines as the quality of surface is the focus. Small blocks of colour, pattern and texture, each trying to

Opposite page: *close-up photographic study of the wing of a tawny owl plus some preliminary observations* (below) *using a range of paper surfaces. Compare the differing marks made by pencil and pastel on contrasting paper surfaces. (Sketch by Shirley Warren.)*

This beautiful study (left) *was worked by Alex Caprara who used gouache and coloured pencils to describe the delicate patterns and subtle tones of the wing.*

achieve a particular effect, will enrich your knowledge of mark-making and, if you note down what you used each time, be useful for future reference.

The beautiful wing from a tawny owl, featured opposite, was taken from a bird killed on a road. A photograph cannot really compensate for seeing it first hand although the tonal variations are obvious and indicate which methods of working might best describe it.

We all see things differently and consequently our drawings will vary greatly. One person might choose to emphasize the movement of the feathers whereas another might find the colour blending more exciting. Alex Caprara, a professional artist, has made a study of the wing in his style. He has used gouache and coloured pencils to illustrate its delicacy with a sensitivity and accuracy that indicates constant practice. Another artist, however, might tackle it in a completely different way.

Whatever our drawing ability we can all make a start by looking closely at objects we enjoy seeing and holding. By reworking the image in a number of ways, not only will we gain knowledge of the subject, but achieve a degree of sensitivity towards the design media which will give confidence in the future.

Candle wax was melted down and, using a sponge, simple shapes were printed on a dyed paper ground. The sponge was dipped carefully into the heated wax (avoiding skin contact) and printed repeatedly. Several prints were made from each dip. When dry a wash of diluted black water-based ink (one part ink to three parts water) was brushed over. The transparent candle wax has resisted the ink and allowed the dyed colours to shine through.

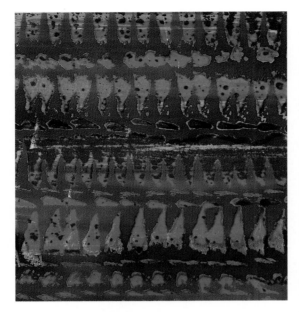

The pattern for this resist was cut from masking tape applied piece by piece and pressed down carefully. At the top of the pattern some masking tape has been left on. After the ink wash had dried each piece was gently lifted to reveal the coloured background underneath.

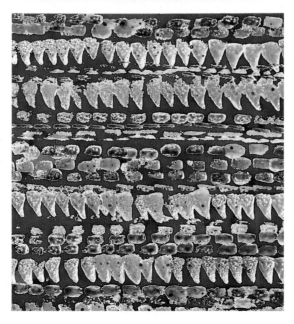

Melted crayons have more concentrated pigments than the candles and when melted were painted to achieve this resist pattern.

RESISTS

There is a wealth of inspiration to be found in embroideries from around the world. These richly embroidered Thai hats feature colourful geometric shapes which form the basis of the simple resists on these pages.

The principle of the resist technique is that a barrier of some kind is applied to a background and colour flooded into the design. It will not penetrate beyond the barrier, if the latter has been applied correctly. With a masking tape resist, however, a little colour sometimes seeps under the edge but, if planned for, this can be most attractive.

Long recognized as a method of patterning fabrics, a wax resist may be used most successfully on paper where it can serve two purposes:
1. To work designs on paper first, which can then be translated directly onto fabric, thus avoiding time-consuming and costly mistakes.
2. As a purely experimental medium to provide inspiration for other techniques.

Wax may be used in solid form or melted down and applied as a hot liquid. To start, simply make firm crayon marks on a not too absorbent paper and then, with a fine wash of ink diluted with water, draw a brush gently and evenly across the surface. If the wash is too thick, or the brush strokes too vigorous however, the wax will break down and no longer resist successfully.

Melted wax opens up further possibilities. The ends of discarded candles or crayons can be melted down in a thick-based saucepan – taking great care to avoid accidents. When liquid the wax may be painted, or printed, onto paper before cooling which gives a lovely fluency to the marks. Alternatively wonderfully stippled textures can be made as the wax begins to dry out.

There is great versatility in the humble wax crayon and it is available in such a range of colours, with both fluorescent and metallic effects, that it is well worth the time experimenting with it.

Richly coloured appliqué (opposite page), decorated with buttons and surface stitchery, worked by people of the hill tribes in Thailand.

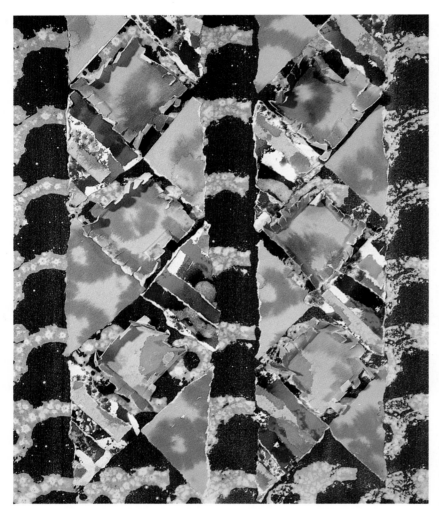

using brushes as the bleach is corrosive and can damage the bristles so do not use a special sable brush and rinse any you do use quickly and thoroughly.

Even when the ink is completely dry the bleach will continue for a while to eat into it so look again after a period of time. Working into a wet wash, the bleach will spread into amazing patterns which may continue developing for up to an hour, although the changes slow down until they are almost indiscernible. Having arrived at these lovely designs, how do you then translate them into images using fabric and thread? Although bleach can be used on dyed fabric and neutralized with vinegar many people are reluctant to risk it because of the long term effects.

Batik, monoprinting and transfer paints could all be used to create very similar images. Instead of eating away at the dye gutta could be printed, or painted, onto a fabric surface and dye flooded in to achieve a similar look. Whichever way they are developed they can inspire highly original textile surfaces.

Ink, paint and bleach were combined to form this abstract pattern (opposite page). Starting with an inked background and bleached prints, further layers were added. It provided the inspiration for a tiny sample of encrusted stitching. (Rona Halford)

Patterns (above) *printed with bleach on ink formed the basis of this pattern. Torn dyed paper was stuck down and then re-torn. (Janet Edmonds)*

INK AND BLEACH

The spectacular and unexpected images made when bleach is applied to inked or dyed surfaces are a constant source of surprise. At first, just watch and enjoy what happens as the colour is eaten away in a totally unpredictable way. After the initial explorations it is possible to work with a greater degree of accuracy. Experience will give you greater skill in developing this exciting method.

Bearing in mind that bleach is a hazardous substance and should be handled carefully, it reacts well with a selection of water-based inks. Fountain pen inks, which react particularly well, can be bought in a variety of lovely colours, such as sepia and turquoise from art shops, as well as in the traditional black or blue available from high street stationers.

A firm cartridge paper makes a good background. Paint a diluted wash of ink over the background and allow to dry. When dry apply the bleach in a variety of ways using the ends of brushes, paint brushes and pen nibs in thin, thick and irregular strokes. Be very careful if

This pattern (right), *taken from an ancient buckle, has been drawn using bleach on an inked surface. Its charm lies in the irregular marks which are possible using this technique. (Gwen Hedley)*

Carton card (above), *with a semi-shiny surface, was covered with a very strong layer of wax and oil crayon to form a heart design. Drawing inks of various colours were brushed very carefully over the surface and left to dry. Then using a sharp tool and delicate touch, directional strokes were etched away, using cross hatching in places, to reveal the pattern underneath.*

small pieces will help to establish a rhythm and movement. The lines may vary in direction or cross each other, depending on the desired effect. Experience will enable you to work with an even pressure so as not to tear away at the surface of the card.

By using the blade parallel to the surface and scraping areas rather than lines a lovely antique look appears. A word of caution – all the little scrapings of dried ink are still very strong and will smudge or spoil papers if not cleared away. Using a soft dry brush gently free the surface of all the speckles and dispose of them so that they will not ruin other pieces of work. With this method some of the crayon colour is lost but further experiments with other combinations of pastels, chalks and inks will offer an even wider range of possibilities.

SCRATCHING INTO SURFACES

There are many ways of scratching through layers to reveal unique textures. A smooth surface, such as carton card, is ideal for this technique as heavily textured surfaces impede the rhythm. Wax crayons have been used for many years in this way, often by children. Start with a pale but thick layer of colour and build up using darker colours reserving the darkest for the top layer. Using a fine screwdriver, or scratching tool, scrape through the layers to reveal the colours underneath, brushing away the scrapings to see the pattern. Initially it may only be possible to work crude images although these may be what you want. Further samples may become more sophisticated. A beautifully subtle design will be made by placing tissue paper over the sample and ironing it. Some of the pattern will melt onto the tissue paper giving two, diffused images. They may be left or brushed over with the most delicate of ink washes for an abstract and subtle effect.

An alternative method is to use a wax or oil mix pastel which is ideal as it gives vibrant colour and some resistance to ink. Cover the card surface with colour in a pattern or image of your choice (in this instance it need not be applied in layers). Paint over the top, gently, with undiluted drawing inks in a variety of colours. Experiment with some of the strong colours available, especially the viridian which seems to add a special luminosity to a design. (Gold and silver drawing inks do not work well using this technique.) When the ink is completely dry use a pointed tool such as a light craft knife to scratch gently away at the ink and reveal the colours underneath. Practice on

Using wax and oil pastels (right) *with a dry ink layer on top, it has been possible to etch away some directional lines indicating how stitches might be worked to recreate a summer meadow.*

The inspiration for this design (opposite page) came from Peruvian art. Dark ink, applied to a paper base, was scratched and scraped away, giving a feeling of antiquity to this modern interpretation. (Denise Waddington)

PAPER PATTERNS

Paper is the foundation of most design work as it is so versatile. This section deals with the exploitation of paper techniques such as printing, manipulation and patterning which will enable you to create your own coloured backgrounds. These designs will be so much more stimulating than shop bought papers because they will be quite unique.

Techniques will be simply explained to encourage experiment. Once again the emphasis is placed on allowing time to play and to explore several methods until a rewarding result emerges. Make that first step and surprising, sometimes vibrant or subtle, patterns happen. With each new experiment you will gain in experience and this will be carried forward to more ambitious projects. All the designs illustrated here have been inspired by the different patterns and colourings of ducks. They are abstract images developed from basic printing techniques – a sponge shape has been used to print and overprint with a mixture of paints and inks, a simple process which is explained on the following page.

Patterned papers such as these could inspire a wide range of embroideries as well as being put to good use. Handmade book covers, boxes, gift tags and wrappings can easily be made. But beware, once your friends and family have been spoiled by these individually designed gifts, they will anticipate future presents with extra relish and you will be kept very busy.

Ingres paper formed the background for the printed papers displayed here as it is fine, strong and of good quality. The handmade notebooks were covered with the paper and the offcuts made into gift tags. Shop-bought gift bags can be opened out and used as a pattern to make your own, which could be constructed from paper, or perhaps Vilene. This can be printed with fabric dyes and stitched for an extra special gift. A decorative envelope for a money or cheque gift can be easily made using a commercial envelope as a pattern. This envelope was made from dyed and printed felt and embellished with machine and hand stitching.

A page of reference (above) taken from a notebook. Based on live and carved ducks it gives details about their colours, feathers, claws and tails – invaluable information for pattern making.

PRINTING WITH SPONGE BLOCKS

Printing is one of the oldest forms of pattern making. A quick look round almost any room will reveal many quite ordinary items which can be used to make a printed mark. These could include corks, pencil ends, pieces of card, string, textured surfaces and, of course, fingers. Many people have failed to realize the extraordinary possibilities of this technique because they were probably introduced to it in a less enlightened time. A familiar school exercise of the past was to carefully fold grey sugar-paper into equal sections and then print very precisely in the centre of each section with a cut potato – the emphasis being on accuracy. Potatoes still work of course and have their uses but at first they are too wet and juicy and then dry out. It is also tricky to cut them perfectly flat. Printing is one technique which can be worked very successfully in the home without the use of specialized equipment. It also works equally well on both fabric and paper.

It is usual, when making prints, to have a dish of paint or ink of a fairly stiff consistency into which the printing block is dipped. The dish

A selection of sponge blocks (right) cut from rubber. The designs, based on duck references, were roughly drawn on the sponge and the background areas cut away with sharp scissors, leaving the raised areas as a printing block. Several colours can be painted directly on a block for an interesting print.

sures the patterns have a special charm and quality.

A variety of repeat prints are easily achieved depending on the colour and wetness, or dryness, of the sponge. Starting with a full loaded sponge and allowing it to exhaust the paint is an excellent way of discovering some of the potential of this method. Overlapping, fading and building up in colour will create free backgrounds which can be worked on later in greater detail.

When printing patterns always consider the shapes the units make in relation to each other as it is the background spaces which often give the design its strength.

The sponge can be washed and used time and time again. Having experimented on paper it will work on fabric although some adjustments have to be made because of the absorbency of the fabric. Transfer paints work particularly well as the subtle printed textures iron off beautifully onto the appropriate material.

Printing is a vast subject to explore and when combined with other methods there is simply no end to the ideas which can arise. This bears repeating because so many people are reluctant to experiment and mix techniques.

Printing works well on multicoloured as well as plain coloured papers. Providing that the background is sympathetic to the printing then beautiful mixtures of shape and texture will inspire future projects as well as giving pleasure at the time. Make careful note of the order of working and materials used. It is almost impossible to recreate exactly, which is one of the joys of creating new designs, but a pleasing result may need to be developed further.

This background paper (centre) has been printed with tail-feather patterns using coloured paints on an ink background with gold overprinting for highlights. The print (above) was made by dipping the sponge block into chlorine bleach (not too wet) and printing onto a water-based, painted ink ground. When dry the bleach ate away at the colour in an unpredictable way. A wash of drawing ink was brushed over the surface for extra depth of colour.

can be lined with a foam pad to absorb the paint and give a more even distribution of colour. It works well if the paint is brushed directly onto the block as it avoids waste and allows more than one colour to be painted on at a time. It also results in more interesting patterns.

The printing blocks featured here and the ones used on the previous page were made from foam rubber, quite the simplest and most effective method of home printing. Its flexibility makes it ideal for using with papers and fabrics as it can compensate for uneven surfaces. It is also textured and by applying different pres-

The robust lines of this group of people (right) were made by placing paper over an inked surface and drawing onto the plain paper with a blunted paintbrush end. When dry the print was placed over a textured surface and a wax rubbing made, further colour was then added to achieve the lively market atmosphere. (Liz Harding)

A bleached pattern (below) has been printed with a stencil onto dyed tissue paper and enriched with iridescent pastel. The background was then overlaid with strips of paper. (Elizabeth Coughlan)

MONOPRINTING

Monoprinting is widely used in design work and it has fascinating applications for fabric (see *Book II – Stitched Images* pages 84 and 85).

A small piece of glass or smooth Formica makes a good base. Rollers or palette knives are useful for applying the ink or paint to the glass.

Initially, printing inks are best and these will be found in oil- or water-based varieties. The water-based ones are the simplest to use from a cleaning point of view and black a good colour with which to experiment.

For the first trial roll a layer of ink onto the clean surface. Then, taking a simple tool, perhaps the end of a brush or a piece of card, draw into the surface. You will discover the marks and textures which work well as you go along, fine channels, for instance, tend to close up when the paper is applied. The nature of the technique necessitates speed and fluency, and this is most important when using acrylic paint and other substances which dry out very quickly.

Having made your marks, take a sheet of fine paper, for example, photocopying or typing paper and place it over the inked surface. Smooth out the paper and apply pressure gently until the image is transferred to the paper. A second much fainter print can also be taken. When thoroughly clean apply more ink and start again.

Another useful method is to apply a layer of

ink which could be textured depending on how it is applied. Place a piece of fine paper carefully over the inked surface and draw on the paper with a blunt tool. The drawing picks up the ink and the paper is patterned by the textured ink.

When dry, inks and paints in differing colours can be applied to enrich the print. There are many colours of printing ink available so that multicoloured prints can also be made.

Paper shapes, cut or torn, and placed on the inked glass give a third variation. The first print will take the form of voided shapes on a textured ground. Instead of cleaning it off roll ink over the paper which will have stuck to the glass for a more subtle design.

Continued experiments will be repaid by the exciting patterns achieved whilst the skills acquired relate directly to monoprinting on cloth with fabric paints or inks.

Falcon on Bow Perch (above). *This beautiful design is actually a yellow-Formica printing block. The surface was inked and paper shapes placed on as a resist. Many prints were then taken and, as printing ink and gouache were rolled onto the block, it became more and more interesting. A print taken from the block* (left) *using gouache and ink. Some of the paper from the block has been transferred to the print but this adds to the effect. (Phil Palmer)*

From left to right: *cartridge paper sponged with ink and pleated when dry. Blue ink dropped between the folds added to the pattern.*
An inked background with melted wax shavings and yellow gouache stippled through a paper doily.
Scrunched and creased wallpaper lining paper was flooded with unfixed procion dye.
A sponged background was folded with overlapping pleats and gouache stippled over the folds.
A dyed background with inks blown across the surface using a drinking straw.
Inks with dishwasher salt dropped onto the surface.
Overlapping layers of printing made using a fairly dry sponge.
To achieve this unusual effect two layers of clingfilm containing wax shavings were ironed between layers of baking parchment.
Scrunched, dyed paper with wax crayon rubbings.

PATTERNED BACKGROUNDS

All the papers pictured here were worked with basic techniques and using only the primary colours of red, yellow and blue. Unusual tonal variations in mixtures of ink, paint and dye record just a few of the things which are possible. There are descriptions of a few tempting starting points but new ideas abound with each sample. Some of the more interesting patterns emerged as a result of a mistake or accident making it even more worthwhile writing notes. Who knows when you might need to recreate something similar?

Keep all the papers, even the ones which at first sight do not seem promising, for instance, coloured newspapers could prove useful. Ex-

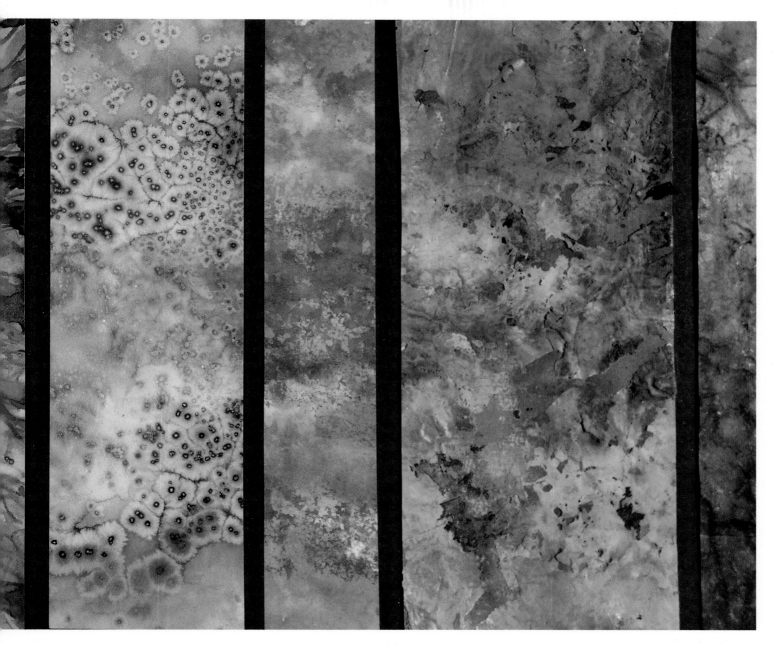

periment using different papers – scrunch them up or fold and pleat them – you will be surprised at the results. Usually the most exciting images are those worked on a really tatty piece of paper which was just a quick try out! On a practical level, it is the cry of many embroiderers that there is not enough space in their homes to accommodate all the materials they need. Having to take things out and put them away each time makes starting even more difficult. The unwillingness to commit the first mark to paper or fabric is a common inhibition but if possible try not to squeeze a first attempt at something new into a few moments between other activities. Overcoming a lack of confidence requires time and organization. If time is short start collecting all the things you might need beforehand, such as newspapers, pieces of foam rubber, plastic, a mouth diffuser and brushes, so that, when you are ready to start, precious time is not wasted looking for things. In this way you are less likely to become disheartened.

As you work, make adjustments by determining if it is too light, too dark, over-busy, heavy or precise. Remember it is much easier to get darker than vice versa so, if in doubt, start with the palest colours and work towards the darker shades.

The more you work the more adventurous the designs will become so you have nothing to lose. If you have an idea try it out and if it doesn't work then note it down as part of the learning experience.

FROM PAPER TO EMBROIDERY

Some people enjoy working with cut paper as a source of ideas. Self-coloured papers will add greatly to their vocabulary. The papers on this page were all developed from drawings of churches.

Following the initial observations and inspired by the qualities and colours of the stone, printed papers were produced by sponging onto a dyed ground. The use of collage to create the final images is very effective, fully exploiting the textures and subtle tonal variations of the prepared papers. Shop-bought papers could not possibly have contributed to these unique images. The final embroidery (right) was worked in such a way as to exploit the atmospheric qualities of the paper.

Imagine the exciting appliqué which could result from fabrics treated in this way, and, as you will see in *Book II – Stitched Images* (see

A design based on a church (opposite page) *with sensitive sponge-printed papers (using poster paints) to create stone colours and textures. (Barbara Young)*

Inspired by the printed papers (opposite), *fabrics displaying this delicate patterning* (below) *have been worked into patchwork samples. These could be developed into larger embroideries. (Barbara Young)*

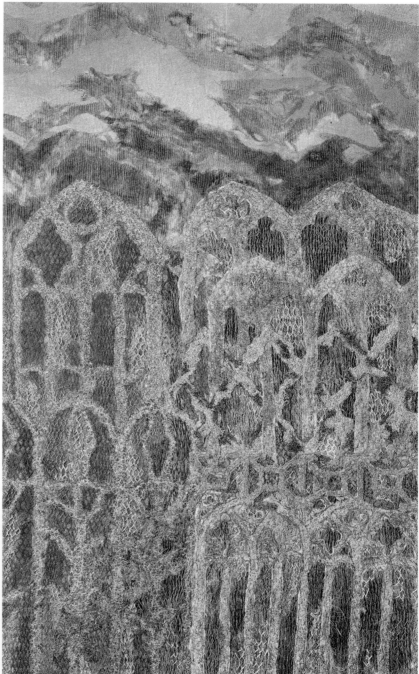

page 92), it is possible to recreate many of these ideas as embroidery designs using the range of fabric paints we now have at our disposal.

That lovely traditional technique of patchwork could also benefit from the array of background possibilities shown here. Plain and patterned fabrics used sensitively in imaginative arrangements extend the scope of this technique enormously. Small, cut paper patterns backed up by fabric samples would serve as a reminder of the possibilities for future occasions.

This embroidery (above) *was again inspired by the quality of the printed papers. Smocking, appliqué, fabric dyeing and machine embroidery have combined to achieve the speckled quality of the paper designs. (Barbara Young)*

MANIPULATED PAPER SURFACES

One glimpse at the array of textures shown here demonstrates just how much richness and variety can be created by using just one colour. Imposing such a restriction focuses the mind on the particular quality you wish to exploit, in this case, paper surfaces. For this experiment colour would have been a distraction.

There are obvious parallels with fabric manipulation, for instance, arrangements of pleats and folds might well inspire the texture on a garment or wall hanging.

The basic philosophy of starting small and building up gradually applies here also. A large piece of paper may be daunting whereas small square, or rectangular, pieces, each illustrating a different effect, are more manageable. They can then be arranged appropriately or indeed kept as samples.

PVA is an excellent glue to use for sticking down such samples as it dries transparent. Whilst the best paper to use for this kind of work is cartridge, an assortment of white papers will add to the possibilities. It may help to jot down a list of techniques to try such as:

cutting	plaiting	weaving
tearing	curling	slashing
scoring	twisting	moulding
pleating	scrunching	building up in layers

Within each method there is scope to vary the scale, proportion and quality of paper.

Following the abstract patterns, interpretations of landscapes can be reduced to white. Of course work in colour adds a new dimension but the appealing simplicity of working in monochrome is a worthwhile and rewarding discipline.

Being careful not to crush the original, photocopies of the textures bring interesting images to light. If you find working in one colour stimulating try making a collection of objects in your colour and assemble them in a glass jar or transparent plastic chocolate box. There will be some interesting juxtapositions and with the aid of a card window small sketches of these patches of pattern can lead to fabric and stitch exercises.

Further experiments using combinations of colours and textures offer a richness of palette that could take a lifetime to work through, and inspire a wealth of embroideries.

Opposite page: illustrated here is a group project where each student was asked to work a number of small squares using paper textures. It culminated in this patchwork of rich textural ideas (see Book II – Stitched Images, page 101).

A moulded and textured paper surface (below left) was inspired by colours and patterns from a bird and in turn proved to be the inspiration for the manipulated fabric sample (left). (Margaret Jones)

A vivacious paper and stitch sample (below) based on a shed window. Dyed tissue and card shapes have been combined with scrim and stitch. (Sue Wilson)

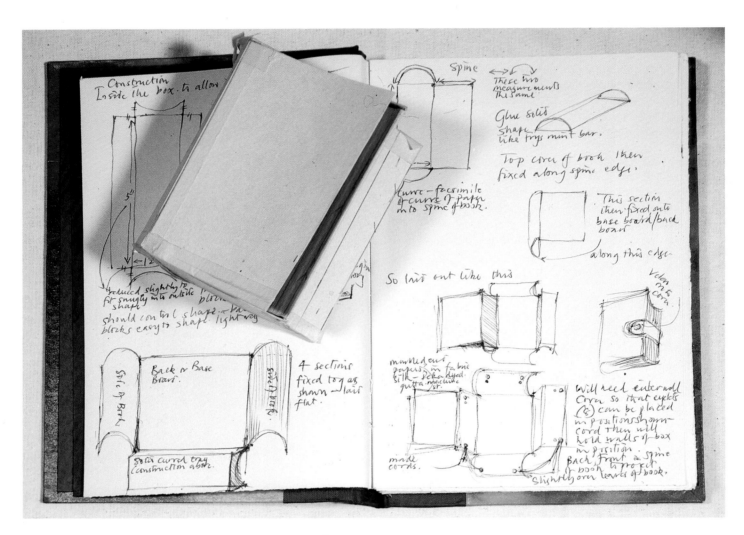

A notebook containing the preliminary sketches for a box (above) *designed to open like a book. By working through the ideas in this visual way they are clarified and a rough card mock up helps to identify any problems. (Shirley Warren)*

BOXES AND BEADS

When time is short there is a great temptation to go straight into an embroidery from an initial sketch and hope that it will work. For some people it does, yet others benefit from solving their problems on paper first and this is especially important when working on constructed items. These can range from embroidered boxes, bags and jewellery through to simple garments. So often they are designed to be seen from one position only, when they would be so much more satisfactory if designed as a whole right from the beginning. How one shape leads to another, simple constructional problems etc become evident as you turn the model in your hands. The mock-up will expose design weaknesses and help organize colour proportions.

This is an excellent opportunity to expand on some of the manipulative techniques seen on the previous page. Quite ordinary ready-made boxes can be used to work out colour proportions as can be seen in the illustration on this page. But for a special box an accurate measured model is still a good idea. Handmade

paper strengthened and embellished with machine embroidery would form the basis of stunning costume jewellery which, for special occasions, need not necessarily be robust. Earring and brooch fastenings can be bought from most art or craft shops.

Beads are easily constructed from paper and are a marvellous way of using all the little patterned offcuts you have been saving. A watered down coating of PVA glue will add strength to the paper although it does alter the quality of the surface leaving it slightly shiny. It also seals the colour into the paper and prevents bleeding if wet.

The fact that there is such a practical application for all the lovely techniques shown here should prove a good incentive to experiment, since it is only through trial and error, selection and rejection that some of the work illustrated on these pages came into being.

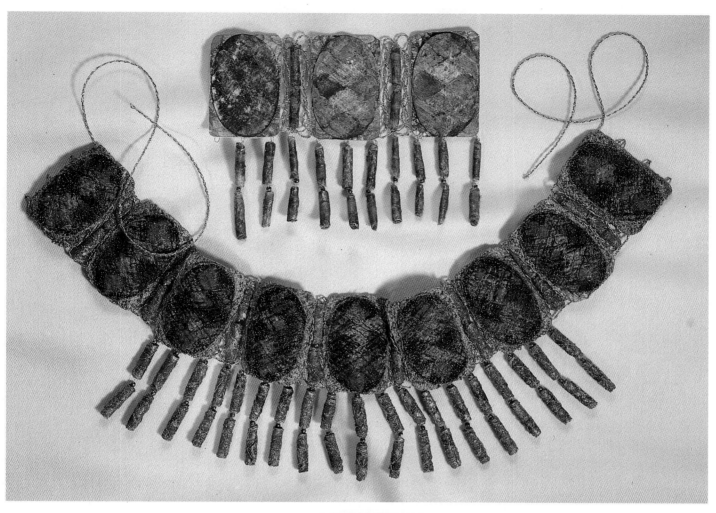

The boxes featured here (right) *started life as containers for a Christmas pudding and a Camembert cheese! They were covered with scrunched up tissue paper stuck down with PVA glue and then painted with drawing inks to create a rich layer of colour. If the box you are using is brightly coloured then it may be wise to start by covering it with a layer of plain white paper. Lustre can be added by gently rubbing in a tiny amount of metallic powder. This method of working could be used to try out ideas for embroidered boxes and, by finishing the inside and base of the box with other papers, would make an innovative gift box. The larger beads were made from dyed paper with a fine layer of PVA added to give strength whilst the smaller, textured tissue-paper beads were wrapped around pieces of drinking straw to give them a rigid structure. (Paper beads by Hannah Littlejohn)*

This delicate jewellery (above) *was first worked in paper ink and paint. The paper beads have a beautiful delicacy which has been fully matched by the fabrics. The design was printed on organza using transfer paints and pieces applied to a water-soluble fabric with free machine stitching. The fabric was then bonded, machined and rolled to form this luscious jewellery. (Lee Foreman)*

MULTIMEDIA DESIGN

One of the great joys of working with fabrics is that they can be worked on many different levels to create pockets of depth or mounds of fabric and stitch. Rich textured surfaces contrast with flat patterned cloth. So when designing for fabrics it is helpful to select an appropriate method which will act as an aid to exploring such textural layered images in a combination of media.

Combining more than one type of material has already been touched on in previous pages but there is no limit to what can be done. Students of embroidery often need to be encouraged to use mixed media and it is difficult to understand their reluctance when they achieve such stunning results. The in-between stage of exploration, ie after the observation and before the actual worked piece, can be the most demanding. Interpreting source material into ideas that are wholly appropriate to fabric and thread is after all the ultimate goal and any technique which will help towards this end is worth pursuing.

We have papers which can be patterned, cut, reassembled and manipulated. The soft textured surfaces made with crayons and wax pastels can be scratched into, but why stop there? Further layers of paint and ink or print may be just the combination to inspire. If not, cutting up and reassembling could prove fruitful. Allowing time to develop different ideas using the same theme is very important and cannot be overstressed. This is the stage where we can make value judgements on composition, colour and tone. Use the application of the media to resolve some of the ideas you plan to work in the embroideries. By tearing, cutting or applying relevant brush strokes, you can determine the type of fabric needed or the direction of the stitch required. Is the whole piece so busy that your point of emphasis is lost? We can all became so absorbed in small areas of our work that we lose sight of the overall composition and end up with a finished piece where the sum of the parts is greater than the whole.

This large design (125cm x 100cm) was worked to scale using wallpaper lining paper. Using a combination of acrylic paint, crayon and Polyfilla, papers were added and then torn back to achieve the distressed look. A great deal of thought and reassembling took place before arriving at this final image. (Denise Waddington)

A large torn paper design (125cm x 150cm) using a variety of magazine and dyed papers (right) *is seen here being used as a working pattern for the embroidery. As pieces are completed they are added to the design to ensure correct tone and form. Once all the parts have been completed they will be stitched together and further stitching added to blend the images together. (Mary Way)*

LARGE-SCALE DESIGNS

The design on the previous page and those featured here indicate a few of the ways in which design problems have been tackled. Everyone needs to find a way of working with an appropriate method which is helpful to them and responds to the challenge they have set themselves. A feature of these particular designs is that they were designed to scale and reasonably large.

In the case of the birds (see previous page), the designer knew the sort of work she wanted to do and set about building up in papers and paints much in the way she hoped the final piece would look. Throughout its progress it changed many times and because it was worked flat against a wall any problems were much easier to see. Working on a table is all very well but proportions can become distorted and it is

not until you see things vertically that you can fully judge the overall balance.

The lively pattern illustrated on this page was based on observations of a squash. A lot of work went into preliminary drawings and design developments before the designer arrived at the idea of combining them into this format. It is not as easy as it might appear to put a few images together in a geometric pattern and hope that it will work, careful planning makes the end result appear deceptively simple.

The bold squash patterns were carried out in a combination of wax resist, flour and water paste, inks and paints. Interestingly enough, the finished design in this case dictated the technique. The textures achieved in this way seemed to convey the essence of the idea so well that any preconceived ideas of techniques were rejected in favour of appliqué, dye and stitch.

When tackling large-scale design it helps to

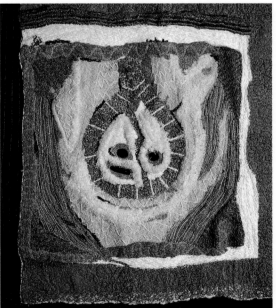

see it, however rough, to full scale before embarking on what might be a very time consuming textile. Smaller working drawings give some idea but not until it is enlarged to full size do the proportions and composition become obvious. What might be an uneasy arrangement of colour and shape when small, may be glaringly offensive on a larger scale.

The traditional method of enlarging is by grid and as a rough guide this works well. Wallpaper lining paper is good for this purpose as it is relatively inexpensive and comes in long lengths. Some people use enlarged photocopies. This involves organization and some expense but if it saves a day of valuable time then it may be well worth it, although sticking the photocopies together to make a large design requires patience. An episcope is a machine which projects an image of the design onto a wall: the scale can then be adjusted according to your needs, even upto quilt size. It is a very useful tool and if a considerable amount of your time is to be spent enlarging designs then it is a very quick and effective method to use.

Large-scale work can be very rewarding and

These vibrant patterns (above) *have been enriched by the application of wax resist, paint and wallpaper paste. The etching on the surface has given added texture to the final design (110cm x 91cm). (Jill Traub)*

This stitch sample (left) *in machine and hand embroidery was influenced by the marks on the paper design. (Jill Traub)*

multimedia designs give the viewer, or potential client, an excellent idea of what they can expect from the finished piece and allows the embroiderer to proceed with confidence.

39

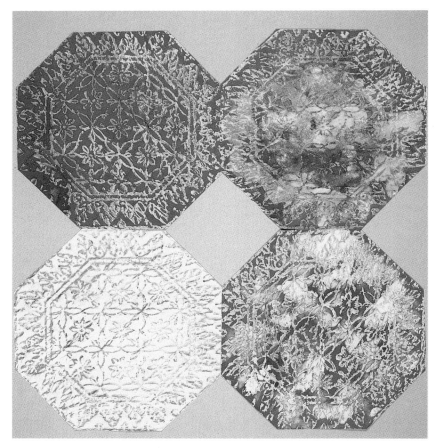

RUBBINGS

Exploring ideas through a multimedia approach is an enormously helpful way of working which will build confidence so that when the time comes to embark on an ambitious project then at least you will have had some experience to draw on. This will lead to a much freer and less inhibited approach.

Take a source which appeals and let it develop, allowing the media to extend the design. A pattern is useful here as a structure to guide you.

Rubbings are a familiar yet versatile technique. Nothing is beyond development, even a method which might be considered dated. It is only a limited vision that might prevent us from developing something new and exciting.

Any hard textured surface may be rubbed, using fine strong paper, with a wax or other suitable crayon. There are examples everywhere from bricks and manhole covers to delicate plant forms. Rubbings are most frequently done on white paper which shows up the textural marks. This same white background, however, might be a distraction when considering it for a design. A wax rubbing will resist an ink wash and look exciting with well-chosen colour

A multicoloured crayon rubbing of a wooden box (above) *was brushed gently with a fine wash of diluted black fountain-pen ink. Small areas of bleach ate away at the surface and drawing inks applied to selected areas.*

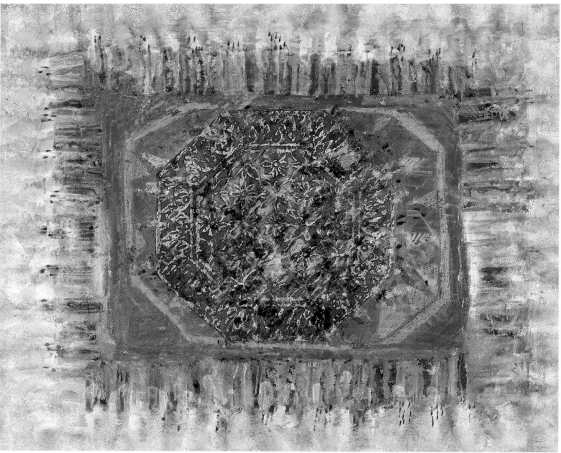

This abstract pattern (right) *grew outwards from the central rubbing, combining wax resist, sgraffito and printed texture.*

Wooden printing blocks and carvings (left), *mostly from India, are both decorative and an excellent source for rubbings.*

A printing block proved the inspiration for a motif cut from sponge and printed in gold onto a handmade paper-ground (below), *coloured with crayon and drawing inks. Further marks and machine stitching completed the piece.*

flooded in. The rubbing itself need not be worked in one colour but a mixture of several which can then be brushed with ink. What started out as a simple pattern has now become a complex image. Details may be emphasized with felt pen or areas taken out with bleach, and when the bleach dries other possibilities may suggest themselves.

This is just one approach: there are many others. For instance, the patterns may be cut or torn and reassembled in new arrangements, with borders and repeats, contrasting in colour and scale by mixing several together. The rubbings need not necessarily be done on plain paper and what wonderfully vibrant patterns this could present.

However timid the designer most people would feel that they could tackle this technique and therein lies its beauty. A simple and accessible approach which is within the grasp of all.

Among the many artefacts from the Middle East now available in shops are wooden printing blocks which have been discarded from the printing process because they are slightly damaged. Besides being decorative they make good subjects for rubbings and can even be used for printing if a receptive surface is available. The rubbings on this page have all been worked with such a block.

Jan Beaney demonstrates how well this technique transfers to fabric and thread in *Book II – Stitched Images* (see pages 79 and 80).

A collage of an old wall (above), incorporating a range of paper, net, bags and burnt plastic, was sprayed with paint to complete the piece (see page 106). (Clémence Gilder)

COLLAGE

spring-clean will have contained everything you need right now.

Collage involves sticking things onto a background. It has a long history and was very popular in the 1960s. It has been associated with bold coarse work, but can be very delicate if used sensitively. As with everything else, the aim is to use the most appropriate materials for the subject. Merely sticking a few interesting things onto a surface is pointless unless they have some reason for being there. They should form part of an integrated design and allowance made for their incorporation. Illustrated on this page we see how a variety of carefully selected materials have been used to develop embroidery designs.

The intricate tracery of a carving in the Victoria and Albert Museum led to the designs shown below. Incorporating string, paper and a variety of colouring media, the essence of the carving, its delicacy and fluidity, has been preserved. These pieces also illustrate the stages of observation and design development required for future fabric interpretation.

In contrast a peeling wall provided the inspiration for a collage of corrugated card, netting, burnt plastic and various papers. Plastic is difficult to paint and the whole design has been sprayed to give it unity.

A simple stone pot with flowers incorporates a variety of torn papers in a free interpretation. Moulded tissue paper and corrugated paper show relief and indicate embroidery options. The touches of complementary colour add the contrast which gives the design its vitality.

We have seen how well paper can be used on raised surfaces but there are, of course, many other things which might be used in the designing process. Plastic of all kinds (for example, the bubble plastic used in packaging), tubing, pieces of string and found objects all have their uses and add further to the embroiderer's problem of what to keep and what to throw away. Storage is a problem and inevitably the box of bits you have just cleared out in the

Guanyin, a carving at the Victoria and Albert Museum, inspired the drawing (right) which in turn led to a string, tissue paper and multimedia collage (far right). (Gwen Hedley)

Moulded and painted tissue paper, corrugated and torn papers suggest that free appliqué might be a suitable fabric medium in which to develop this design (opposite page). (Willemien Stevens)

APPLIED TEXTURED SURFACES

If a substance is thick, malleable and of the right consistency to be applied with a spatula, palette knife or a stiff brush, then it is capable of being fashioned into the most marvellous textures. A little time spent viewing an artex ceiling, however boring, will nevertheless demonstrate the possibilities of such textures which are an important element in the design vocabulary of embroidery techniques.

There are a number of substances that can be used to create textures and only by trial and error will you find those which suit you. For the background it is advisable to use stiff card – a cornflake box would be fine for this purpose. Disposable plastic lids make excellent mixing dishes. Most of the substances will eventually need to be mixed with some form of colour or painted over when dry.

PVA adhesive can be squeezed directly onto the surface and trailed into a pattern through the nozzle at the top of the tube. It may also be applied evenly to the surface and scraped or patterned using tools or pieces of card. It dries transparent and shiny but can be painted when dry, or colour added before application. (For beautiful interpretations of this technique using fabric see *Book II – Stitched Images*, page 80.)

Acrylic paint when textured or imprinted gives excellent surfaces. Some people use it directly onto fabric despite its stiffness.

Flour mixed with water into a stiff paste has many uses. Add paint or dye and apply a layer to a surface. Patterns can then be 'combed' through the paste to create rhythmic shapes. When mixed with a heavy concentration of paint or ink, flour and water paste makes a usable thickener for printing, adding a textural dimension to the pattern.

Gum arabic mixed with colour and spread over card should be left just long enough to harden slightly. It then becomes easier to im-

Opposite page: *textured samples. From the top:*
acrylic paint applied to card and textured like rough icing on a cake.
PVA glue squeezed through the nozzle on the top of the pot created this trail pattern.
Gesso applied to a card surface with a palette knife formed the base of this textured surface.
Flour and water paste was allowed to harden and imprinted with a decorative circular pattern. When dry, ink was added which caused the paste to soften and slide against the background. It is a delicate surface and, burnished with ink, has a subtle richness.
The background to these samples combines all the substances, applied in layers, and scratched back with coats of ink and paint.

print and make patterns.

Gesso is a refined plaster which is available from art shops and sold in powder or liquid form. The liquid is easy to handle and lasts well if the lid is always screwed tightly back on. It has a soft flaky texture when dry, as you would expect, and spread finely recreates distressed surfaces which suit some styles of work. There has been a tendency for it to be over used but that should not prevent its use where it contributes to the integrity of the design or embroidery.

Various glues can also create good textures. Samples should be left to dry before working further.

Textural metal thread work is an example of one technique where work of this sort might prove inspiring. Some of the samples pictured here have been worked with metallic powders available from many art shops. The labelling states quite clearly, however, that they should not be inhaled, but with careful handling they are useful for working rich and lustrous surfaces.

It is possible to achieve great subtlety within a textured surface as shown by this marshland image (above). *Gesso was first painted onto paper then watered down with PVA glue. The design was completed with iridescent crayons and an ink wash. The beautiful embroidery which resulted from this can be seen in* Book II – Stitched Images *(page 120). (Louise Ellis)*

...the hair was grey blue...

LEARNING TO LOOK

There is so much to see around us and so little that we really look at. Close observation enables us to see quite ordinary things in an extraordinary way. Ideally we should all draw a little every day as even the most competent drawers become disheartened when out of practice.

Where do we begin to look? Things close to hand, primary sources that we can handle or observe closely from different angles and have continual access to are ideal. Something which is special to you or that you find has visual appeal will be an encouragement.

The use of a card window to select areas is the tried and tested method which works well for those who are feeling their way. Move it around until you find an area of interest. Attempt to draw what you see using a pen, pencil or fibre tip. Experiment with the media until you find one which suits you. With a pencil there is a great temptation to rub out but in this sort of drawing it doesn't matter if the sketch lines remain as they are part of the learning process. A pen can encourage a more confident approach. Colour information may be added with pencils or any medium of your choice. Aquarelle crayons are particularly useful here and small blocks of colour in a palette at the side of the page can be picked up with a brush and water (see caption on page 12).

As confidence is gained, a sketch to establish the overall shape might be helpful but there is no need to fill in every detail as you will already have that information in your small studies. Many people find the most efficient way of recording information is to combine sketches with written notes. The test of sound drawing is how useful it would be if your source material were to be removed and you had to rely on it.

This method is particularly useful when visiting a museum or exhibition. Useful equipment for such a visit might include a magnifying glass, a camera with very fast film as flash is often forbidden, a portable set of colouring media and a tape measure to ascertain scale. With this basic equipment a visit will be as profitable as possible.

This is a mounted sheet of a student's work following a museum visit. The students were asked to select a non-textile item from the museum which really appealed to them and study it. (Gwen Hedley)

Where do we find sources of inspiration? It is not easy to focus on an idea which will be totally absorbing and sometimes it may be necessary just to make a start. An obvious place is in the home. Carvings, jewellery, ceramics and treasured objects provide opportunities for making rubbings, pattern and texture. Look at them closely, perhaps for the first time, and be prepared for some surprises. Small areas out of context may reveal exquisite details previously unobserved especially when seen under a magnifying glass.

Progress onto groups of items within the home sometimes deliberately, at other times casually, placed. Isolate areas by means of a card window and don't attempt the full 'still life grouping' for preliminary studies.

Why not try the bathroom, with its pots and tubes of toiletries and brushes, or the kitchen with shelves piled with tins and packaged goods. Even the odd packet past its sell by date might have some use in a composition. Plates of food, leftovers, trays of eggs, kitchen utensils, an overloaded ironing basket or washing line, may inspire if looked at with vision and imagination. It really does not matter where the idea comes from the main thing is to make a start and, however unlikely the source, the possibilities will escalate the more you work on them. Anything can be made special and unique if you spend a little time exploring it – a fact which cannot be over emphasized. So when in doubt, don't sit around waiting for inspiration to strike like a bolt of lightning but make a positive start with something close to hand.

It works well for many to have a focal point on which to concentrate and develop. The source can be varied. A colour, a pattern, a texture or a word can set the mind off down paths of discovery. It is such a relief not to keep saying, 'What shall I do now?' In this way the more you think about it the more varied the ideas and there are times when thoughts race on far faster than your capacity to develop them. Make a habit of writing them down to look at later.

Some ideas, inspired by the home, which might deserve a more in-depth study could include:

My favourite things
A quiet corner
Table settings
A room of my own
My family
Nooks and crannies
An indoor garden

Jewellery has such a wealth of pattern (above) *that it is easiest to start off by examining small areas with a card window or under a magnifying glass. There is no need to draw the whole thing if it is a repeating pattern. Establish the overall shape and add details and notes where necessary.*

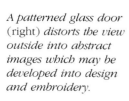

A patterned glass door (right) *distorts the view outside into abstract images which may be developed into design and embroidery.*

These, and many other subjects, which you can think of, will give more opportunity for thought, resulting in new and imaginative interpretations.

Distortion in the home is a complex starting point but one which fires the imagination. Think of your own home and all the places where you might find distorted images. Reeded glass offers enticing flashes of colour and rivulets of pattern which are quite special. Steamy and rainy windows also cause distorted views and will necessitate quick sketches which may be all the better for their urgency. Observe the curious reflections in kettles and other rounded shapes which act like the distorting mirrors in a fairground. Car bodies, reflective surfaces such as tin foil and metallic wrapping papers, all provide ideal sources. There is no end to the possibilities which abound once you become aware of them.

Don't be inhibited and remember that distortions are a step away from the reality of the actual image. Your interpretation can therefore be much freer. Imagine the fluid colours which might be used for silk dying as a result of these studies.

Observe flower stalks in a glass jar and consider how they might inspire exciting linear motifs. It is a subject which could go on and on. You could set up your own distortions by placing colourful objects in front of metallic paper and record the results.

If this idea does not appeal there are innumerable other themes such as curves, grids and contrasts which might set you off onto a new and rewarding design area. Exploring your home with fresh eyes cannot help but awaken awareness of the tremendous potential of a familiar but perhaps underrated source and nothing will seem quite the same again.

Sea urchins (above right) *in reflective surfaces display subtle distortions. By drawing small sections some new ways of looking at familiar objects will emerge. Very bright objects may produce startling and original designs. Experiment with the papers and angles and try to organize a group which can be kept in position for some time so that you may look at it from different angles.*

These subtle colour studies (right) *resulted from shells reflected in different metallic surfaces. By placing them between folds of wrapping paper with a grid, delightful patches of pattern came to light which suggested these innovative fabric interpretations. (Shirley Warren)*

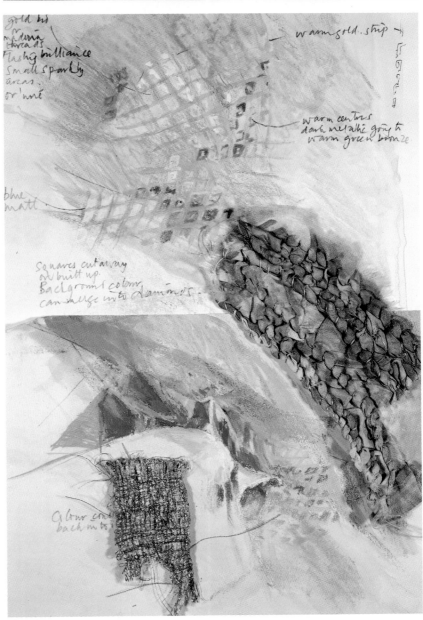

FURTHER AFIELD

Once you start to think of ideas beyond the home it becomes almost overwhelming and even more necessary to focus your mind on an idea or theme to structure your looking.

The holiday might be the only time when you have a real opportunity to sit and sketch and therefore your time must be used efficiently. Photographs make an excellent background reference but, when confronted with a new situation, it is so easy to shoot off pictures indiscriminately at anything which takes your fancy and yet fail to find what you really need to help with your design work.

A good tip to make your photography both more interesting and worthwhile is to have an angle of some sort. It might be a favourite view seen at different times of the day or seen from different levels such as lying down and as high as possible. You might decide to home in on pavements and floors, or look up and explore skies. The act of selection will help your critical faculties and inspire purposeful looking. You may also find that it gives you greater pleasure. It naturally follows that drawing can be treated in much the same way and, if time allows, will ultimately prove more useful than photography.

It is not necessary to travel too far from home

to find images which will inspire exciting designs. A shopping trip or walk with a pram can indicate any number of subjects to exploit. Beautiful plants can reside next to decaying walls and graffiti. There is a general and very valid concern for our environment which is a good reason why it might inspire textile design. They may not, however, contain the picturesque subjects or decorative images using precious materials that the general public has come to associate with embroidery. Instead the fabrics may be ripped and torn and, perhaps because of their vulnerability, prove an excellent medium for describing urban decay.

Looking at the ground with its litter, rusted and crumpled drink cans and discarded wrappings can be demoralizing. Why not use them as a design source and a way of making a statement? A response to the theme 'Found on the ground' could give rise to an amazing combination of colourful and abstract images. Embroiderers constantly use discarded materials in their textiles and the theme 'Rubbish' could be looked at both visually and practically as a good way of encouraging the recycling of materials. Embroidery should reflect current ideas and attitudes of society if it is to be accepted as a valid form of expression. Walls covered in graffiti can be deeply offensive but undoubtedly reveal exciting colours and textures. In an urban environment there are often illegal posters piled one on top of another as a result of the unsuccessful efforts to tear them down. Attempts to draw and record these lively images can prove embarrassing but the urge to record something potentially exciting will spur a determined embroiderer on at the risk of family ridicule.

What one person sees as litter another might visualize as a marvellous starting point for an embroidery design. Silver foil (above) tarnished from a barbeque and a discarded drink can, offer interesting patterns for imaginative quilting, appliqué or hand stitching.

The randomness of graffiti (left) could prove a unique source of pattern and design. A promising area could be isolated and used as a repeating motif. The whole image could be worked on paper and then on fabric with resist techniques.

The distressed quality of this old wall (opposite page) exhibits a subtlety of surface that would be a great inspiration for hand or machine embroidery. (Clémence Gilder)

LOOKING THROUGH

Having established that a theme liberates us from the continual problem of choice, its development depends greatly on how we pursue the ideas once we have decided upon our subject. So let us take an idea and consider some of the ways in which it might be expanded. 'Looking through' is a possible theme. Unlike the previous page where 'Urban decay' was the topic, this subject does not indicate an attitude or approach. It is very open and could be interpreted in any number of ways.

Looking through what? This is the first question we might ask. Could it be man-made or natural forms? Let us take leaves as an example. They can be at eye level on a bush or up in a tree making shapes against the sky. In the spring leaves burst forth in strong acid greens sporting vigorous growth whereas in September they are vivid yellows, pinks and reds in a tired configuration. Some leaves grow in an orderly form which frames an enticing view and others grow so profusely that they all but mask the landscape beyond.

If you have ever tried lying on the ground and looking through the grasses to a distant scene, you will know that it may be uncomfortable but well worth the effort for the new perspective it gives you.

Hedges provide natural grids through which you can see fields and meadows carefully divided into new shapes and patterns. Indeed,

Looking through the natural forms of rhubarb leaves (above). *(Elsie Probert)*

A simple sketch of trees (right) *seen through the mesh of a net curtain indicates several ways in which this image might be developed to produce a fresh look at a familiar subject. (Angela Poole)*

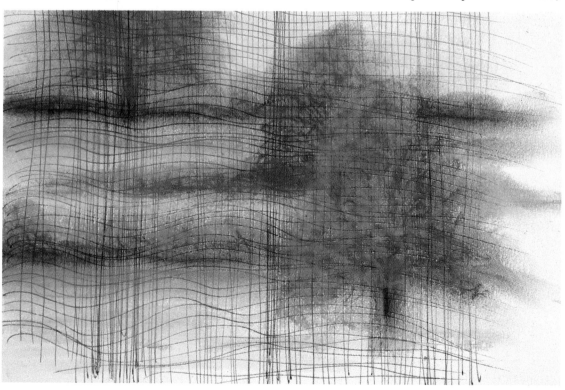

man-made grids could be another aspect to explore, for instance, a garden seen through a wire mesh, a fence or a trellis offers a new dimension to a familiar subject.

We are also faced with the interesting dilemma of which aspect to concentrate on, the barrier or the view beyond the barrier. This gives tremendous scope for interpretive designing. Exaggeration of the aspect which appeals to you will make it unique and special.

'Looking through lace curtains' conjures up a visual image and hints at the secrecy of the furtive watcher behind the curtains and the image of the curtains as a shield.

Seeing the world compartmentalized by leaded windows might lead to innovative patchwork.

Looking at the fleeting images of the landscape through an aircraft or car window, or the seaweed and sand beneath rippling water, makes us re-evaluate how we look at things. Moving images such as these are difficult to draw so use words to describe what attracted you to look at them.

Archways, bridges and railings create a natural frame for embroideries if care is taken to interpret the observation in an appropriate way. It is always tempting to work the embroidery so that it replicates the original as closely as possible and not exploit the fabric's properties. It is the essence of the subject that should be the motivating force and not a fabric and thread facsimile, and we should be aware of this when making our observations.

Once a subject has become a real passion the ideas present themselves in an ever more diverse form. 'Looking at the world through rose-coloured glasses' could present an opportunity for a humorous or a serious study. 'Through a keyhole' has sinister overtones but it could lead to straightforward observations. 'Through the looking glass' provided Lewis Carroll with an amazing vehicle for inventive thought and this is what a really stimulating theme should offer. Look upon it as a springboard for the imagination – with its roots in sound observation acting as the spur to invention.

Following studies of trellis and plant forms several variations were tried in paper and paint to interpret the idea of 'Looking through a trellis'. The resulting stylized pattern (above) *has a crispness and vitality based on observation which at the same time fully exploits the fabric techniques. (Angela Poole)*

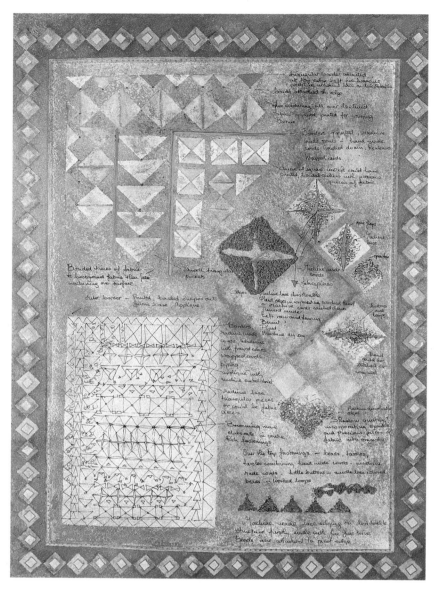

A notebook page (above) *full of information and ideas. Set out sequentially it illustrates how the design has been developed. (Clémence Gilder)*

a methodical way and others dot about. Many work on rough paper and stick the pieces in if that is a way of working they find comfortable. What matters is that you keep your material in such a way that it is convenient and useful, as these books are central to design development. There is no need for others to see it. Pen and pencil might not be the most promising way of recording ideas for you, so another medium, torn paper for example, could be used.

It is a good discipline to stick in samples of the appropriate fabric and thread with the ideas for your future reference. Most of us know far more techniques than we use and samples stuck into a sketchbook jog the memory and encourage us to expand our vocabulary.

It is essential to keep a special and accurate record of dye samples as these are notoriously difficult to reproduce. Ideas books can be simple statements of visual observation with comment or demonstrate a wide use of media. Some people take the opportunity of using the book itself to further the development of ideas by colouring the pages or placing the drawings in a patterned or sequential way.

Select the sketchbook thoughtfully for your type of drawing. The paper can vary from thick watercolour to thin cheap paper. Ivorex board books are expensive and limited in size but they are excellent for thick textured drawings as they stand a considerable amount of punishment.

Photographs stuck in for added information have their place and with the odd magazine cutting form useful backgrounds but they don't compare with your own drawings.

A visit to an exhibition or degree show is often stimulating because of the stunning workbooks. The thought processes behind the finished pieces are a fascinating visual account of an attempt to develop ideas in a unique way. You may be surprised to note that it is not always those with the more accomplished graphic skills who have the most exciting notebooks. With embroidery it is the ability to turn observation into a valid textile image which is the overriding factor in determining success and ideas books play a vital part in this process.

KEEPING AN IDEAS BOOK

It can be called a sketchbook or a notebook, it really doesn't matter as long as it contains the information and designs which might inspire an embroidery. It should be a unique collection of drawings and thoughts assembled in a style suited to the person using it. There is no right or wrong way and some will be neat and organized whilst others will be scrappy, chaotic and full of bits and pieces thrown together.

It is not necessary to keep ideas in a book. Pieces of paper kept in a file or portfolio can serve the purpose. Bound sketchbooks, however, are a disincentive to tearing the pages out and in so doing prevent it from becoming a polished but not necessarily useful aid to design.

Some people work through from page one in

These torn paper shapes of chickens (above) *are deceptively simple. Based on observation they have been thoughtfully placed to inspire further work. (Phil Palmer)*

A sketchbook (left) *bursting with visual information worked in torn paper and fabric samples. (Willemien Stevens)*

EXPLORING IDEAS

As more design confidence is gained there is often a desire to incorporate more than just a visual image and infuse an essence or spirit into your work. This is not always easy and it may be helpful to have some approaches which will assist you. The temptation to be too literal is always there because of the comfort of familiar images. Indeed there are those who aim to achieve a near photographic picture with their embroideries. The textiles which really excite many of us, however, are those which celebrate the unique qualities of fabric and thread. But why use fabrics? What is it about fabrics which so excites us? For many it is the tactile properties, the richness of surface or the manipulative potential. So how may ideas be best expressed through this medium?

There are no complete answers, merely options and, in the next few pages, we will consider some ways in which we can take ideas further by thinking beyond the obvious and by providing a framework of reference for those who might wish to explore abstract imagery.

The development of a theme offers just such a structure and it is hoped that by demonstrating a variety of solutions to a given challenge, you may find ideas which will help you with your own work.

The subject 'Scapes' is vast, including as it does, townscapes, landscapes, skyscapes and seascapes. Each one is capable of infinite variety. The townscape featured on this page was inspired by crumbling buildings in a Cretan landscape. It describes the scene and conveys a sense of heat and decay. Initial sketches in a holiday sketchbook provided the information which made possible design ideas when the holiday was over. A number of explorations, each one attempting to reproduce a sense of place was followed by a full-scale mock-up in dyed and torn papers including tissue. This was the most appropriate method of describing the decaying houses in sunlight and shadow. Composition, colour and balance were established in this way before embarking on the embroidery with its added dimension of textured surfaces.

Cretan buildings worked in free appliqué with dye and hand and machinery embroidery to soften and blend the shapes. (Eileen Goldschmidt)

SCAPES

Photographs may well help to establish a location and give photographic accuracy but rarely do they convey atmosphere. A sketch, however brief, is a much more personal statement carrying the stamp of being there.

When pursuing a theme like this you might consider the following: what is the essence of feeling behind the images you wish to describe? Write down words or phrases which convey the atmosphere or spirit of the view.

Aspects to take special note of could include weather conditions, intensity of colour, texture, line or pattern. The weather in particular might indicate an atmosphere; perhaps overcast, brisk, oppressive or bright. Would the view be better described as dramatic, harmonious, welcoming, peaceful, calm, exhilarating, friendly or even threatening? Are the features craggy, sharp, barren, sparse or lush, smooth and tranquil? Just one of these words could lead to an interpretation evocative of the spirit of the 'scape'. Search out colour references which take the image beyond the mundane. Exaggerate, if necessary, to enrich a hue which captures the mood. Colours beguile our senses and help us to feel as well as see.

What first attracted you to this idea? Is the memory now faded or immediate, larger than life, vivid, in and out of focus or distant?

When drawing, consider the scale. Epic views may need space to establish a reference point.

You may find passages from poetry or literature which reinforce your own impressions, or music to stimulate an enlightened response to what you have seen.

All of these thoughts are an aid to you in your search for appropriate methods of expressing your ideas in a visual form, if you remain receptive.

Which are the most apt media for describing harmony and tranquillity? Would they be the same if it were a harsh threatening image? Probably not.

You will find that new ideas will flow once

It is hard to identify any specific image within this design (above left) *but somehow it manages to convey a sense of landscape and tranquillity. The initial observation was followed by several designs before arriving at this atmospheric interpretation. (Reni Tajima)*

Hot colours using pastels (left) *indicate an exotic location. Colour can be all important in establishing mood. (Mary Way)*

A gentle watercolour study (left) *of an English landscape with masking fluid resists to enrich the lines of movement in the growing crop. The marks have been simplified and hint at stitch or fabric interpretation. The colour blending is sympathetic to the way in which silk fabric paints merge and this method of designing was chosen with that in mind. (Elise Lynch)*

In contrast to the gentle movements of the landscape (left) *there is dramatic feeling within these simple marks describing a wild moor* (below). *(Barbara A. Woolner)*

you have become totally absorbed in your subject. Experiment with different design techniques to see which one best satisfies your thoughts. For instance, try several colourways and analyze which one best enhances the mood. Should your image be depicted as one panel, or one of a series, separate sections, pieced work, split images, or a combination of scales within one piece?

It may be that a mixture of ideas within one design is the ideal way to express your feelings. Remember that your original idea was there to inspire and not restrict so you have every right to exercise licence if it promotes an idea. With total immersion in a subject and familiarity with the imagery your interpretations will become more confident and enable you to make your subject unique and special to you.

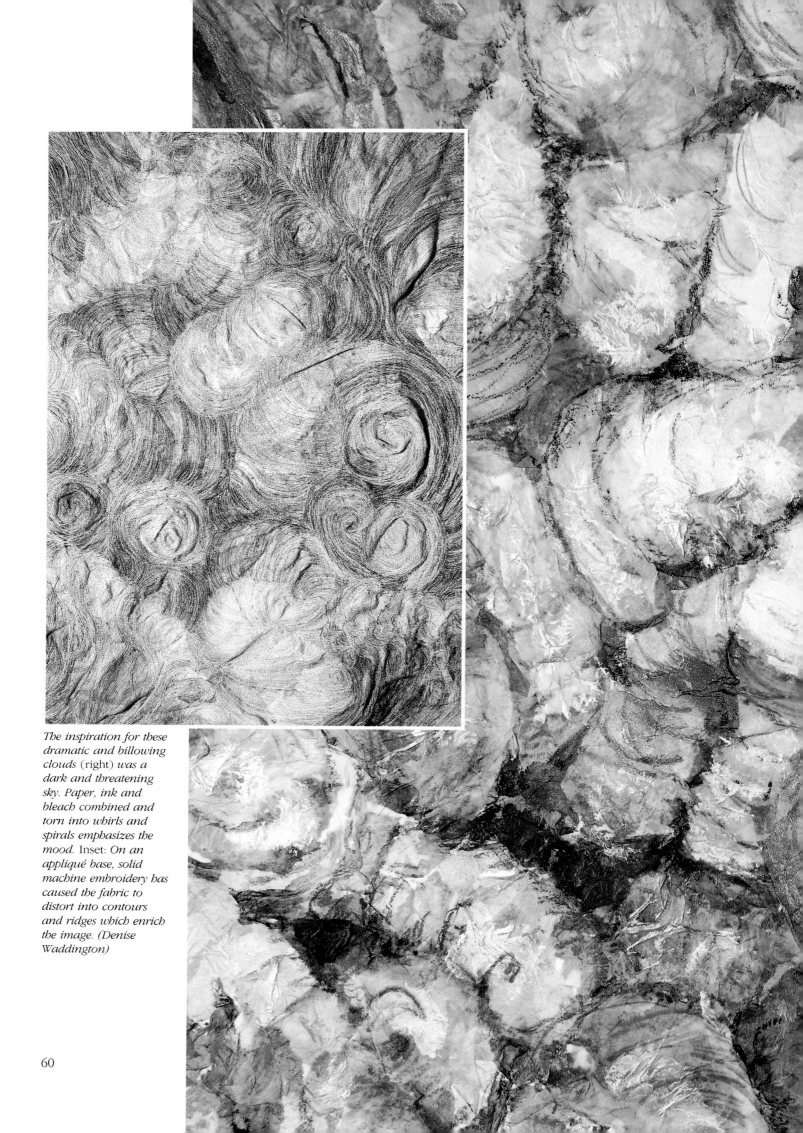

The inspiration for these dramatic and billowing clouds (right) *was a dark and threatening sky. Paper, ink and bleach combined and torn into whirls and spirals emphasizes the mood.* Inset: *On an appliqué base, solid machine embroidery has caused the fabric to distort into contours and ridges which enrich the image. (Denise Waddington)*

This rich and dark evening sunset (left) *with rolling, moving colours has been achieved by blending inks and paints to create a smooth flowing design. (Carolyn Walker)*

An English sunset (below) *provided the inspiration for this delicate embroidery. Lightness was achieved by layering delicate stitched fabrics on a handmade paper ground whilst directional stitches blended the shapes and added emphasis. (Judy Henderson)*

61

Pages from a sketchbook (right) *with primitive patterns derived from African art. Using procion dye as a paint, bleached away and ink lines added for detail. (Willemien Stevens)*

A pattern, derived from an African source, freely drawn (below). *(Willemien Stevens)*

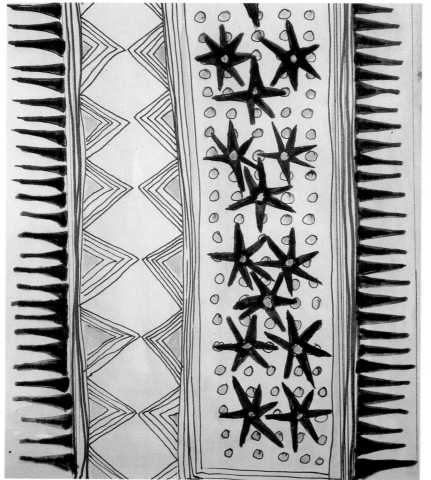

PATTERNS – A POSSIBLE APPROACH

Without a focus pattern is such a huge area that it would be daunting to tackle. Since earliest times pattern has enriched most aspects of our lives. It has become a popular source of inspiration for contemporary embroidery design as is evidenced by many recent exhibitions.

When you consider borders, corners, repeats, asymmetry, symmetry, tessellations and random patterns are just a few of the areas of design potential then a personal approach becomes very desirable. We can invent patterns, or look around us at those which appeal, and adapt them to our purposes.

The designs on this page were made in response to a group project on 'Patterns from the Third World'. It was first necessary to ascertain which countries qualified and with help from Oxfam and the Commonwealth Institute these were established. Then each student was asked to make original sketches of artefacts from the country of their choice and for this many found the Museum of Mankind in London very useful.

For the first design session they were asked to bring in all their normal drawing equipment and so it was to their great surprise that initially they were asked not to use any of it. It seems likely that the patterns they so admired were made by simple and often primitive tools and

so it was inappropriate to start with highly sophisticated design media.

Their first task was to go into the grounds and find anything which could be used to make a mark. Twigs, pieces of bone, mosses and grasses became the drawing tools. Instead of sharpening pencils it was twigs honed down to make a mark or frayed out to form a brush, or grasses tied together. This encouraged great ingenuity and was an effective way of utilizing the environment. Extracting pigment from the soil did seem a bit extreme so the colouring media was their own!

The marks made with these resourceful tools were fascinating and quite different from those that might normally be expected. They were irregular, sometimes coarse and other times sensitive but always unique.

The linear designs were followed by printed marks with paint, ink, dye and bleach. The highly individual and often unexpected patterns achieved in this way formed the basis of design development for an extended and successful project. The initial spontaneity promoted a fresh look at some old ideas which were then developed in a wide variety of ways. The group also gained support and encouragement from each other.

Whatever the design source there are always new ways of attacking it with vision and imagination so do not be deterred from developing something which appeals to you because you think it is being done by others. Just remember that with thought and inventiveness you can find a new and rewarding way of making it your own.

Following studies taken from an Indian pattern a number of designs were made each one becoming more abstract. This pattern (above) *was worked in paint on a textured tissue-paper background. (Linda Scott)*

Developing the theme 'My favourite things' this student has made a representational study of a group of objects which have special appeal to her (right). It is interesting to see just how much of the flavour of the original still exists in the design (far right) which is a photocopy of the original cut up into strips and reassembled. Another cut photocopy of the original (below), this time woven together, gives tantalizing glimpses of the figurative design although it is more abstract than the previous strips. (Rona Halford)

ABSTRACT IMAGES

When working in an abstract way there are few points of reference to fall back on when things are not going well. Of the many approaches that can be made there are some guidelines which offer a framework and therefore security to start you on your way.

Select an image from your sketchbook and trace or photocopy it. (This is one occasion when the creative use of a photocopier can save lots of time.) Try cutting the image into strips and rearranging them in a variety of ways. Change the order as you put them back together again. Change the levels so that the shapes distort. Tear strips and have some narrow and others wide. Use a card window to isolate areas which have potential. The strips need not be placed vertically and weaving them together fragments the image even further. If you have made several photocopies then you can try all these ideas and stick them down onto a background for further working. Even though the designs have undergone major restructuring it is amazing just how much of the flavour of the original is retained. The designs can be coloured and details added. More drawing may be needed to give a clearer indication of an image.

Fabric transfer paints on paper backgrounds can be cut up and reassembled in this way as you can see from *Book II – Stitched Images* (see page 84).

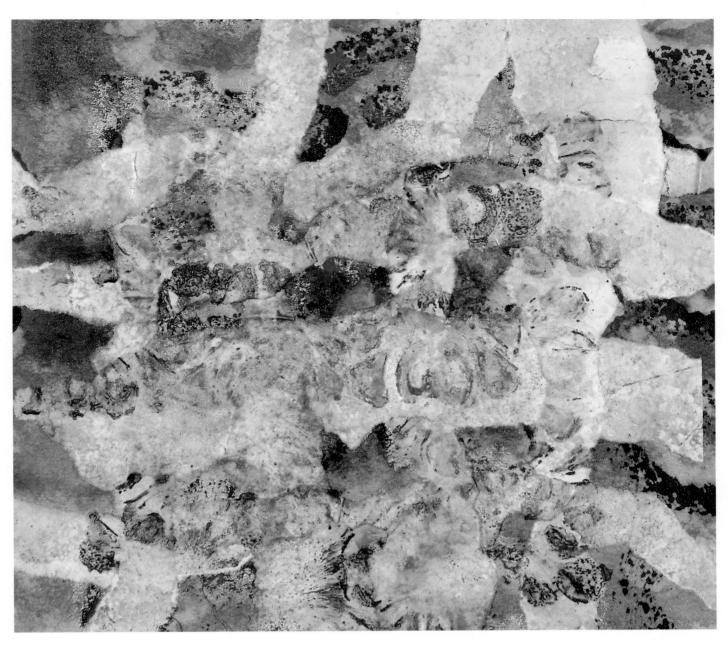

Other possibilities might include mixing more than one scale in a single design. By enlarging and reducing on a photocopier this process is considerably speeded up. Cut up both a large and a small image and alternate them. This will take the design even further from reality and yet again if you mix two entirely different drawings together. However far fetched they may become you still have the original to refer to if you wish to restore order to the design.

Tracings may be taken on a layout pad, easily acquired from an art shop. The paper is not as transparent as tracing paper and excellent for exploring design ideas. When placed over a drawing most of the strong lines are visible but the fine details will be slightly less defined. This can be helpful if you wish a less literal image. With subjects such as landscapes and gardens, where there is a temptation to draw in every petal and leaf, a less precise drawing still records the proportions and movement but encourages a more free interpretation. It is also far easier than looking through half closed eyes. Pages in the pad can be overlaid so that new developments can be worked on an existing drawing without the need to redraw.

Photographs may be cut up into strips or squares, reassembled and redrawn through tracing or layout paper, thus revealing unexpected combinations of shape and colour. You will find abstract images almost without thinking and this may set you off in an entirely new direction.

This lovely abstract design (above) *has been made by tearing strips and weaving them together, drawing and painting on top with inks, poster paint, gold powder and iridescent pastels. It is interesting to note that the original source of inspiration was an 'Art Deco' design. (Elizabeth Coughlan)*

A close-up of the tree texture (right) *on a paper ground shows french knots in a thick silk which have been machined into so they were absorbed into the overall texture.*

A tree-bark texture (opposite page, left) *created using dyed tissue papers torn back and crayon marks added for emphasis.*

The decorative border of a Turkish towel (below) *featuring a repeated tree motif.*

TREES – A PERSONAL THEME

Everyone tackles their own work in different ways but for many working from a theme is the way in which they can best structure their thinking. New techniques and images can be slotted in to expand the evergrowing bank of ideas. Embroidery is such an exciting area of work, encompassing as it does so many different facets, that in a lifetime we can only hope to scratch at the surface. So much the better then if we can concentrate and develop ideas as thoroughly as possible and get as much out of them as we can. If there is a limited time to work ideas then you will carry your knowledge from one to another and not start again with each new piece. It can become an obsession often with family involvement.

Ideally it is best not to force ideas but allow them to develop naturally. Ready-made ideas for embroideries do not often lie in wait for you, more often than not you will have to work hard to arrive at suitable designs. Never underestimate thinking time as it is through this process that ideas are sifted and rejected. A notebook close by in which to jot down your thoughts will ensure that they do not get forgotten.

The following study of trees illustrates this point – it is a brief diary of the thoughts and ideas they inspired over a two year period.

A subject for a theme can arise from any source, but, in this case, it came as a suggestion from a friend who thought it would be interesting to see how four people would tackle the subject and then exhibit their results. To have a goal is a great incentive as it is so easy to waste time unless there is a deadline and this can focus the mind particularly when the finishing date approaches. If you feel that you need some incentive to get a series of work done but have no group with whom to exhibit then try booking something like a local building society window or library entrance and work to a date either on your own, if you are feeling brave, or with friends. You will be amazed at how much work you can produce and how fast it will develop when you have given yourself this pressure.

Trees are a good primary source as they are accessible and prolific. You can touch, see and draw them as you wish in a variety of weather and light conditions.

The preliminary sketches were purely for information with colour notes and written details.

One particularly appealing aspect of trees is that they have great strength but within their sturdy trunks you find fragility and delicacy. It was this mixture of roughness and delicacy that provided the first ideas of how it might be developed into a fabric surface. Time was spent seeking out those trees in which these qualities were exaggerated. As the project progressed the urge to describe trees in an abstract textural form rather than as a pictorial image grew. Samples were worked in order to achieve this quality of surface using an appropriate medium.

Visits to museums, and galleries offered opportunities to study trees in textiles, ceramics, stone and wood whilst research revealed that they were once looked upon as possessing life giving properties. The concept of the 'Tree of Life' proved a rich source of visual imagery.

Tree Celebration – *handmade paper pulp pressed onto bandage gauze, dyed and layered, forms the base of hand and machine embroidery* (right)*. The paper softens with working and this adds to the textural feel.*

A set of bark drawings (right) from Cretan trees, torn and reassembled into an abstract arrangement overlaid with a stitch sample showing a possible interpretation. The drawings were worked in Aquarelle pencils of various types.

Another piece slotted into the puzzle with the handling of embroideries from the Middle East depicting this 'Tree of Life'. The fascinating combination of coarse fabric with silk and metal thread found in Turkish towels suggested ways in which they might be incorporated into a modern embroidery. The idea of combining old ideas with new ones was very appealing.

The exploratory fabric samples were beginning to represent the desired quality of surface incorporating texture, coarseness and fragility. This was achieved by bonding a variety of fabric scraps onto a delicate scrim background and machining into the surface in such a way as to blend them and make them part of a unified whole. This formed the cloth into which hand stitching was worked. This extra dimension was needed for emphasis. Rich but subtle textures was the aim and there were many attempts to find this quality before the final method was formulated. Many ideas were tried and rejected on the way. Even ideas that do not work have great value as pointers to new paths.

Paper formed the base of some resolved pieces and with them came the idea of working

in a long thin format. Handmade paper – soft and fibrous – worked onto scrim was remarkably resilient and withstood a great deal of handling and stitching. Indeed the paper softened as it was worked and the qualities were enhanced because of it.

The desire to work large pieces and yet retain a long thin format was bound to cause problems until the idea of incorporating strips of semi-formal tree pattern, inspired by the old embroideries, arose. Using this device it was possible to combine strips into a larger resolved piece of work (left). With another embroidery this formal pattern formed a border round the edge (opposite page). Finally, as it seemed appropriate, fringing was used to complete the piece.

As you can see from the thought processes involved, the finished pieces shown on this, and the previous pages, evolved gradually, combining textures from local trees, colours from exotic Aegean species taken from holiday sketches and patterns from old embroideries. The work hangs freely, its gentle undulations

suggesting the movement of trees.

If starting now things might well have been done differently but such is life. All that we can expect of ourselves is that we do the best we can in the time available. You would certainly work this theme in quite a different way and this is the joy of embroidery. Capable of infinite variety it is the effort to make it special to us that makes it so worthwhile.

Rich textured tree-bark patterns (opposite page) *worked on gauze bonded with fabric scraps. Free machining with a darning foot and no frame caused the fabric to distort and follow the ridges of the bark. This is one example of a situation where you can have an idea but when working allow the fabric to evolve in your hands. The semi-formal border incorporates Turkish 'Tree of Life' patterns. A second textural interpretation* (right) *where scrim has been bonded with colourful fabric snippets and stitched by hand and machine to create a rich fabric surface. The whole piece comprises elongated pieces joined together by means of vertical 'Tree of Life' motifs.*

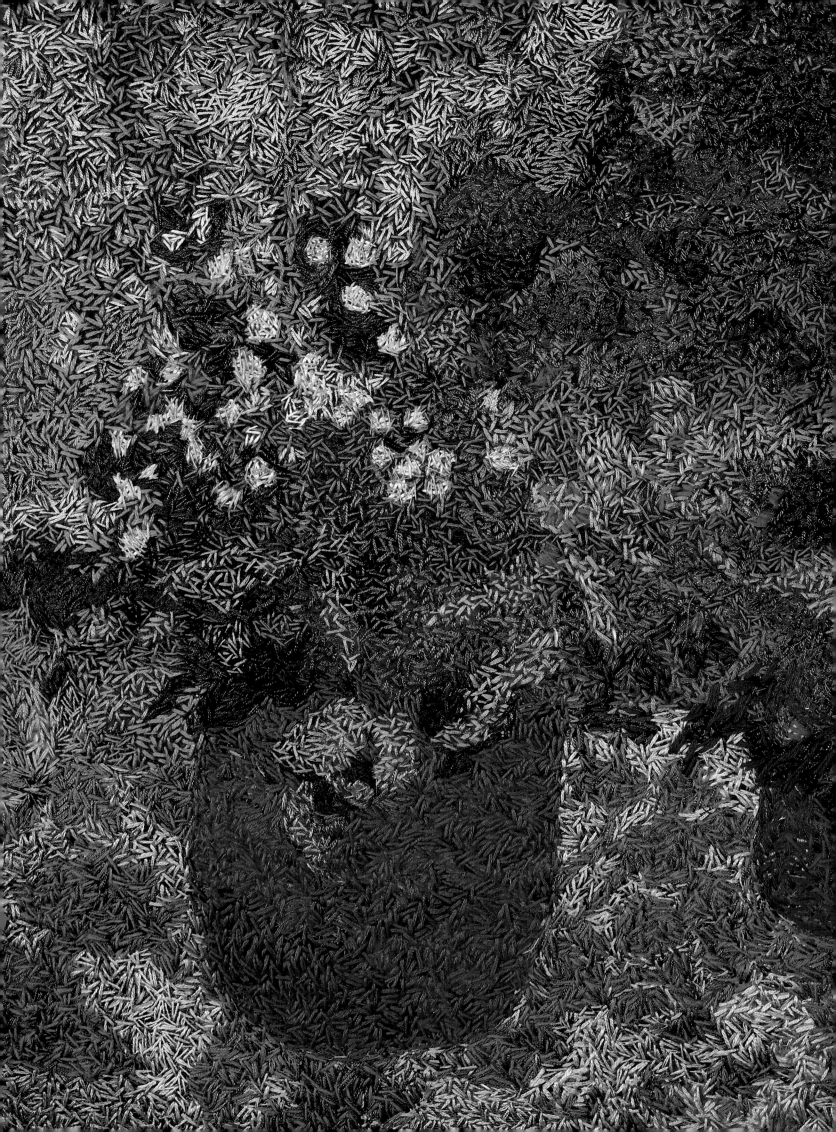

STITCHED IMAGES

Jan Beaney

Above: *detail of figure by Phil Palmer using an unusual method of darning incorporating appliqué.*

Opposite page: In the Shaded Courtyard *by Audrey Walker. This splendid panel is worked entirely in straight stitches using a variety of yarns.*

Previous page: *detail from* Freedom *a panel by Julia Caprara.*

CONTENTS

INTRODUCTION

This book has been planned to follow on from Jean Littlejohn's *Design to Embroider*, complementing or suggesting further adventures into the world of stitches. Although continuing the process of looking, selecting, recording and developing your design ideas, greater emphasis has been put on their interpretations in fabric and thread.

Selecting an appropriate background cloth in colours sympathetic to your design should be one of the prime considerations. If a suitable material cannot be purchased easily there are now many ways to colour fabric using easy, effective methods within a home or studio workspace. Some of the suggested approaches you may wish to revise, rediscover or experience for the first time.

Developing and creating a unique backcloth for your stitched imagery is continually fascinating due to the wide range of fabric now available and because the traditional boundaries of appliqué have been extended.

The interpretive, tactile and thoroughly absorbing activity of hand and machine stitching adds a further dimension and quality of surface which demonstrates quite unique and intriguing characteristics.

Last but not least, the final section combines all these elements. The satisfaction, learning skills and creativity which evolves when finding and working an individual theme is often outstanding. It is a simple philosophy which can be followed by anyone interested in creative embroidery.

Above: *paper and fabric appliqué, coloured using permanent metallic fabric paints and decorated with machine embroidery, by Judith Ann Peacock.*

FABRIC PAINTS

There is obviously a wealth of plain, coloured and patterned fabrics to be found in the shops many of which would be an ideal choice and eminently suitable for many of your projects. However, knowing how to achieve the range of effects which can be created with fabric paints may save you many frustrated hours of searching in your local shops for that illusive shade of colour. You will be able to create your own uniquely coloured background for your stitched project.

A wide range of products are now available and can be purchased from some department stores, haberdashers or suppliers of art materials. If you have difficulties obtaining them, suppliers lists in books or specialist magazines will give you details of the many craft shops throughout the country, many of which offer a mail order service (see page 142).

The paints and crayons selected here have been chosen as they are easy to use in your home and work areas. They are water soluble, easy to mix and to apply. They are all transferred or fixed onto the fabric by the heat of an iron. Other methods and products are available but in some instances expensive specialist equipment or less convenient fixing procedures are needed. Each process described in the following pages offers its own unique characteristics. One paint will produce a particular type of mark or quality whereas another offers a different result. Experimentation and experience will help you to choose the appropriate one for your work.

Designs developed with transfer paints or crayons are transferred from paper to the cloth and can give both clear cut shapes or overprinted textural images. This method does not affect the surface quality of the cloth. Silk paints offer a wonderful range of colours which merge and blend but there is a limited control over their spreading qualities unless gutta (see page 90) is applied to separate the colours. Permanent or metallic paints can be applied directly onto the cloth, their thicker consistency allowing hard-edged designs to be retained, although the fabric has a slightly stiffish finish. The new fabric paints, designed for airbrush use only, also stiffen the fabric slightly.

This picture shows a range of fabric paints now available along with some of the equipment mentioned in the book, for example, glass for monoprinting, masking fluid, card combs etc.

Embroideries from East European countries inspired the patterns (above) used for the card shapes. Rubbings were made with the transfer fabric crayons and printed onto polyester cotton.

TRANSFER FABRIC PAINTS AND CRAYONS

These paints and crayons have been designed to be used on synthetic fabrics. Patterns can be painted, printed or applied to paper which is then ironed to transfer the design onto the cloth. This process also fixes the colour. Many people feel happier and more relaxed painting or crayoning their design on paper first, rather than taking the risk of applying fabric paint directly to the material. Subtle, unusual affects can be achieved through the use of overprinting. The colour print has no build up of pigment to affect the surface of the cloth or to interfere with the enjoyment of stitching into it. Disappointing results can be due to trying this method once, not entirely successfully, and not allowing yourself time to experiment and play with the medium.

By considering the following suggestions, many potential problems can be overcome. The paper should be smooth, polished or non-absorbent. Thin cartridge, typing, computer or photocopying paper have ideal surfaces.

Beware of recycled paper, although commendable in principle, it is sometimes too absorbent for this particular method.

Using a pencil, trace or sketch your design onto the paper, if appropriate. Alternatively paint, print or crayon your patterns. Whatever mark you make whether stippled, drybrushed, splattered or swirled paint, almost the exact image will transfer. Applying the paint with a variety of brushes, sponges, scrunched up kitchen towel, twigs or any other item you think appropriate, will give an assortment of textures. Remember it will print in reverse so, if the need arises, turn the design at the pencil outline stage. Use thin layout paper or hold your drawing up against a window to redraw your design on the other side to eliminate the problem. All colours can be mixed together to make exciting hues and with practice dark, subtle colours can be achieved. Crayons can also be layered to create new tones. Dilute the colours with water if a wash effect is desired or use colourless thickener to pale a colour without affecting the consistency if you plan to print the design. Unusual patterns are printed onto fabric if the design is ironed when very wet paint has just been applied. However, in general always allow it to dry otherwise small, very dark tones print off and spoil your design. A hairdryer is always useful to speed up this process. If crayons have been used shake off any excess powder to prevent spotting occurring on the cloth.

Printing the design onto the material appears to be the easy part but this stage is often hurried. Allow the iron to heat up to the temperature which suits the selected cloth. If in doubt, increase the heat a little as the paper will give some protection. Take time to apply the heat paying attention to all areas particularly the sides of the pattern. Move the iron gently taking care to hold the paper still to prevent the image blurring. Never leave the iron in a stationary position as the shape of the iron and the steam holes if present will show quite distinctly. Still holding the paper securely peep under each corner in turn to ensure an even print. Some designs which are not exhausted on the paper can be ironed again for a fainter, softer image. More paint can be applied to the same design for further printing.

Very bright, sometimes coarse colours, print on synthetic fabrics which could be absolutely appropriate for shadow quilting or certain appliqué projects. The colours will print less harshly, however, on material containing both synthetic and natural fibres. Polyester cotton or polyester viscose will both give good results. Synthetic velvets, metallics and sheers are also effective, but do allow yourself time to experiment so you become familiar with the colour variations obtained on the different fabrics. A clear solution called cotton finish is now available for applying to cotton cloth which should make it easier to apply the paint, although tests have not been conclusive. To summarize, select the correct type of paper and fabric which should be washed free of any 'dressing' and most importantly take time to iron the design carefully so that a full even image is transferred.

The transfer fabric crayons are cheap, cheerful and effective. First impressions suggest a limited colour range but several colours crayoned one on another can result in exciting colour combinations. To familiarize yourself with their potential carry out some simple exercises. Take each crayon in turn and colour several squares varying the pressure of your crayoning to achieve dark and pale tones. Try solid colouring, diagonal or scribble shading.

This delightful work (left) shows the ground fabric printed with fabric paints and decorated with straight stitches worked in stranded cotton and coton à broder. (Anne Jones)

Fabric transfer crayons were used to take rubbings (below) which were printed onto polyester cotton and then backed with felt and stitched with tiny seeding stitches in metallic yarns giving a quilted effect. (Judith Ann Peacock)

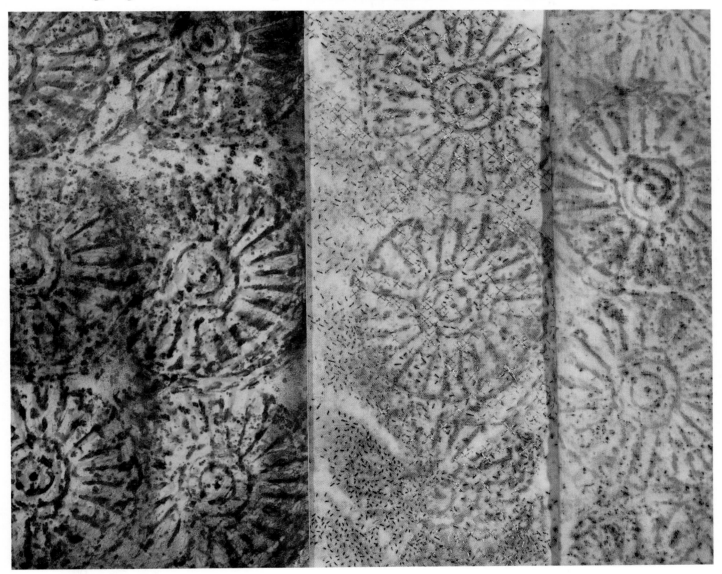

Follow this by systematically applying one colour onto another. Notice the difference if a yellow is put on top of a red and vice versa. Variations will be achieved by printing the colours on different fabrics.

Taking rubbings is a much loved activity although these days some people suggest it is an old-fashioned method. It has always been useful to help appreciate textural surfaces but fabric crayons have revitalized the pastime. Surfaces to be found on walls, pavements, fences and tree trunks, or on household items such as carved ornaments or furnishings can all be the source for taking superb multicoloured rubbings. Sections of these can be printed directly from the paper onto fabric. Alternatively, the pattern could be improved further by crayoning or painting directly onto the rubbing or by applying an all over colour wash. Remember to choose carefully the order of your crayon colours. Dark green, blue, purple and black can dominate your design if applied last.

Marvellous results can be achieved by cutting up your rubbings and reassembling them into patchworks, assorted strips, frames within frames or woven patterns. Before the ironing process, painted and printed papers can also be integrated with the rubbings.

You can also create your own surfaces for taking rubbings. Card shapes can be cut out and glued onto a background in symmetrical, asymmetrical, abstract or figurative arrangements. Cartons or cereal packets would be appropriate materials to use. Initially, place a trial arrangement of thin card shapes. Gently place the paper over them to enable a rubbing to be taken. Adjust, rearrange, add or eliminate the shapes. When you are satisfied, glue the card pieces onto backing card (a strong PVA adhesive would be suitable to withstand the friction of the rubbing action). This permanent pattern will enable you to take limitless rubbings changing the colours, tones and overprinting. Card shapes which have been pasted with PVA glue, embossed wallpapers or other textural material could provide further variations. Repeating units, overprinting or other compilations could be readily tackled in the comfort of your own work place.

Rubbings and fabric prints (top) *were made from these very simple PVA blocks.*

The tree image (left) *was built up with layers of PVA on card to create a printing block for permanent fabric paint. Successful rubbings were also taken using fabric transfer crayons. (Judith Smalley)*

PVA glue applied to card can provide further exciting patterns. Begin by pasting a layer of adhesive on the card. If it is too absorbent and the glue appears to sink into the surface leave this first layer to dry in order to 'size' or seal the surface of the card. Even this supposedly smooth surface will often provide interesting rubbings. Follow the sizing procedure by applying enough glue to allow you to make an impression in it. Different implements will give varying results. The end of a pencil, brush, skewer, twig or card strip would all be suitable. Swirls, waves, crosshatching, flowing and geometrical images can be drawn. If your particular brand of PVA is too runny allow it to dry a little before you begin etching your patterns. The white solution will appear transparent when dry.

Follow this stage by taking a trial rubbing using a soft pencil or crayon. If certain parts of the design need to be accentuated, build up the image with a little more glue. For other linear effects apply the glue from a container with a nozzle, or decant it into a plastic bottle with a pipette or fine nozzle fitted to the lid. Well-defined built-up lines, stripes, blobs and outline shapes can be drawn onto the card and, when completely dry, wonderful textural and coloured rubbings can be made using the transfer crayons. These rubbings can then be ironed onto the cloth.

RESIST PRINTING WITH TRANSFER PAINTS

MASKING FLUID

Designs can be lightly sketched in pencil and overpainted with watercolour art masking fluid. When dry apply the transfer paint, brushing or sponging the paint lightly across the surface. Interesting effects are achieved with some part of the design resisting clearly whereas other parts appear to be washed with colour. Other qualities occur if the imagery is painted with the transfer paints first and the masking fluid painted on top. It can also be rubbed away using a putty rubber or finger so do experiment to enable you to build up a dictionary of marks and textures which could be useful to you for future projects.

Photocopies, washed with transfer paints, surprisingly result in the original black line printing acting as a resist on the fabric. Fine lines only give a faint tracery whereas bolder lines and solid areas show up more clearly.

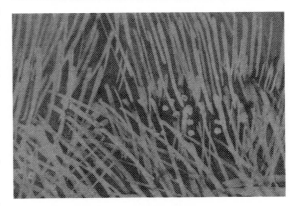

A pattern taken from a Polynesian Tapa cloth inspired this simple design (left) *which was painted with masking fluid before the addition of transfer paint. The painting of grasses* (middle left) *was completed before masking fluid was applied resulting in a softer look. The remaining examples show an image of grasses printed on cloth* (below left) *and a stitch interpretation* (bottom) *worked in straight stitches and couched threads.*

PAPERS

Paint, print or sponge colour over several sheets of paper and leave to dry. Place cut or torn paper shapes, strands of thread, plant material etc onto the fabric. Position the painted paper face down on top of the fabric and iron to transfer the colour. The particular items placed on the material will act as a resist and will be depicted by white silhouettes. Overprinting in a variety of colours with different arrangements of shapes will produce an amazing assortment of patterns. Take care to consider whether the shapes are sympathetic to the proposed design. Hard-edged shapes would be suitable for an abstract grid design but may not be appropriate for a more impressionist picture.

Painted and patterned papers can be cut and placed colour face down before positioning other painted papers on top. In this way an amazing number of patterns can be created. A little more time may have to be spent on the ironing process to allow the heat to penetrate all the layers of paper. Grids, frames within frames, patchworks or floral patterns can provide a challenging basis for stitching.

WAX RESIST

Some types of transfer fabric paints are more fluid than others. This may be a limiting factor for textural or block printing but would be advantageous for use with wax resist. Household candles can be drawn with a variety of effects on paper, an activity many of you will remember from junior school. A white candle mark is difficult to distinguish on white paper unless looked at in a certain light. However, a short time experimenting on scrap paper will help you gain a little more control. Faint pencil-marked shapes or patterns could help as guide-

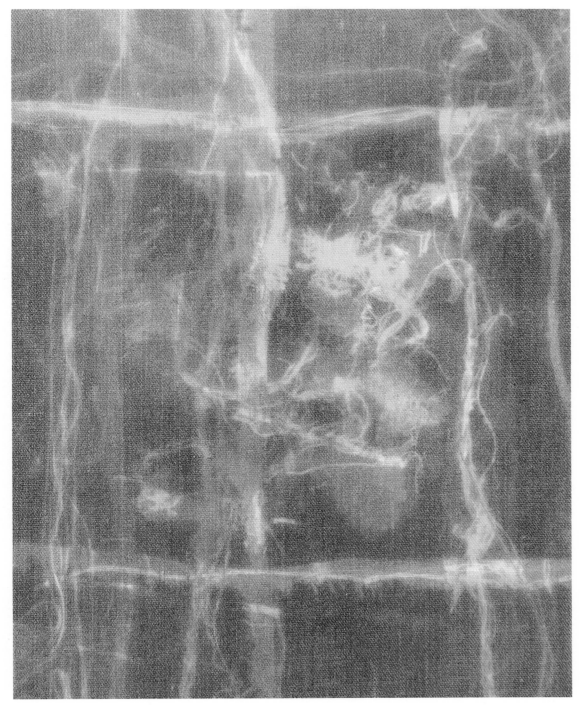

This richly coloured cloth (opposite page, top) *was created by printing with different coloured transfer-painted papers. Flowers, leaves and paper shapes were first placed on the fabric surface to resist the colour when it was ironed* (opposite page, right). *The accompanying photographs* (left and opposite page, bottom left) *show how interesting resist effects can be achieved using a variety of materials such as threads and ferns.*

lines. Remains of coloured candles may give you a pale-coloured mark.

On completing the waxed imagery gently sponge or brush a thin or diluted solution of transfer paint (using an assortment of colour) over the top. Do not make the mistake often found in school projects where thick powder paint was applied over the wax and surprise registered when the wax did not resist the paint. Ink would have given a better result. So do remember to dilute the transfer paint if necessary. Leave to dry.

To iron the design onto the fabric, place layers of absorbent paper such as kitchen towel on the ironing surface. Place the fabric and inverted design on top and cover with more absorbent paper. The heat from the iron will transfer the design from paper to fabric and melt the wax away as well. Specialists will probably prefer to use this batik method directly onto the fabric with other fabric paints and dyes but the unique quality obtained using this method may be just the appropriate mark needed within a design.

These interesting transfer painted monoprints (opposite page) *were created by using a variety of card shapes, pencils and other implements to score textural masks into the paint before the print was taken. Some of the patterns were further embellished with stitching in fine silk threads.*
First row: single rosette chain stitches (left).
Second row: Running stitches in silk and metallic machine threads (left). *Third row: running stitches in silk and metallic machine threads* (left) *and clusters of cross stitch* (far right).

The fabric print (below) *was taken from paper coloured by paint left in a mixing plate. It was then reassembled into a grid and transferred to the fabric.*

PALETTE PRINTS

Printing from your mixing plate or palette can often result in a surprising, colourful and satisfying pattern. On completing your planned design work, never wash the plate or mixing palette free of excess transfer paint until you have pressed or printed every drop onto a piece of paper. Any of the following suggestions could produce unexpected and exciting images.

1.   Press a sheet of paper onto the palette, lift and replace in another position until you have covered or partially coloured the paper as you think appropriate. Leave to dry.

2.   Use up the remaining paint by sponging the colours onto a sheet of paper overprinting one colour on another as you wish.

3.   After blotting off the more liquid content with paper, draw patterns into the remaining skim of paint using the end of a brush or a skewer. Images and textured marks can be drawn into the paint very successfully in the same way as print makers draw into printing ink. This approach is developed further in the following section.

While the prints are drying allow time to look at and possibly develop further certain aspects. You may wish to add additional prints, colours or other details with paints and crayons. Remember that the last colour or mark added can sometimes print on the fabric in an over emphasized way.

Exciting designs can be achieved by cutting up strips of paper and weaving them one into another, cutting out repeat patterns or creating haphazard arrangements before finally ironing them onto the cloth.

MONOPRINTS

The experience gained from printing the left-over paint from your palette will encourage you to attempt more ambitious projects. Many of you will be familiar with simple monoprinting, well it is now possible to print similar images onto cloth with transfer fabric paints using this technique. This is due to the fact that the paints available today are made of a much thicker consistency than their predecessors which makes this a viable and exciting method to use.

Start on this project as if embarking on traditional printmaking. Protect all surfaces with newspapers or polythene. Find a sheet of non-porous material such as Formica, Perspex, industrial polythene sheeting or a sheet of glass. (The latter produces the best results.) Remember to cover sharp edges with insulation tape for protection. Brush, sponge, or roll a thin layer of fabric paint onto the surface. Remember not to be too generous with the paint otherwise, when you press the paper down on the glass, it will smudge and break up the indentation and blur the drawing. If in doubt blot off the excess before drawing into the skim of paint. Using a variety of implements such as a card comb, knitting needle, cocktail stick, kitchen towel or cotton wool bud, score or wipe into the colour to create yet another set of resist marks. Use one colour only for your first experiments in order to discover a range of effects that can be achieved and could provide a useful start to your pattern making. Remember that the image is reversed from glass to paper but prints back to the original view on printing the image from the paper to the material.

Obviously there is an element of chance as there is no way that you can be totally sure of the end result, which is what makes the method so challenging and surprising. Practise the preliminary mark making exercises. This experience, coupled with your knowledge of the transfer paints so far, will help you eliminate the element of chance. You will create unique qualities that might suggest landscapes, water, flower gardens, a field of poppies etc and these coloured backgrounds will make inspiring starting points for design developments. Consider whether adding further paint or crayoning would enhance and develop your design.

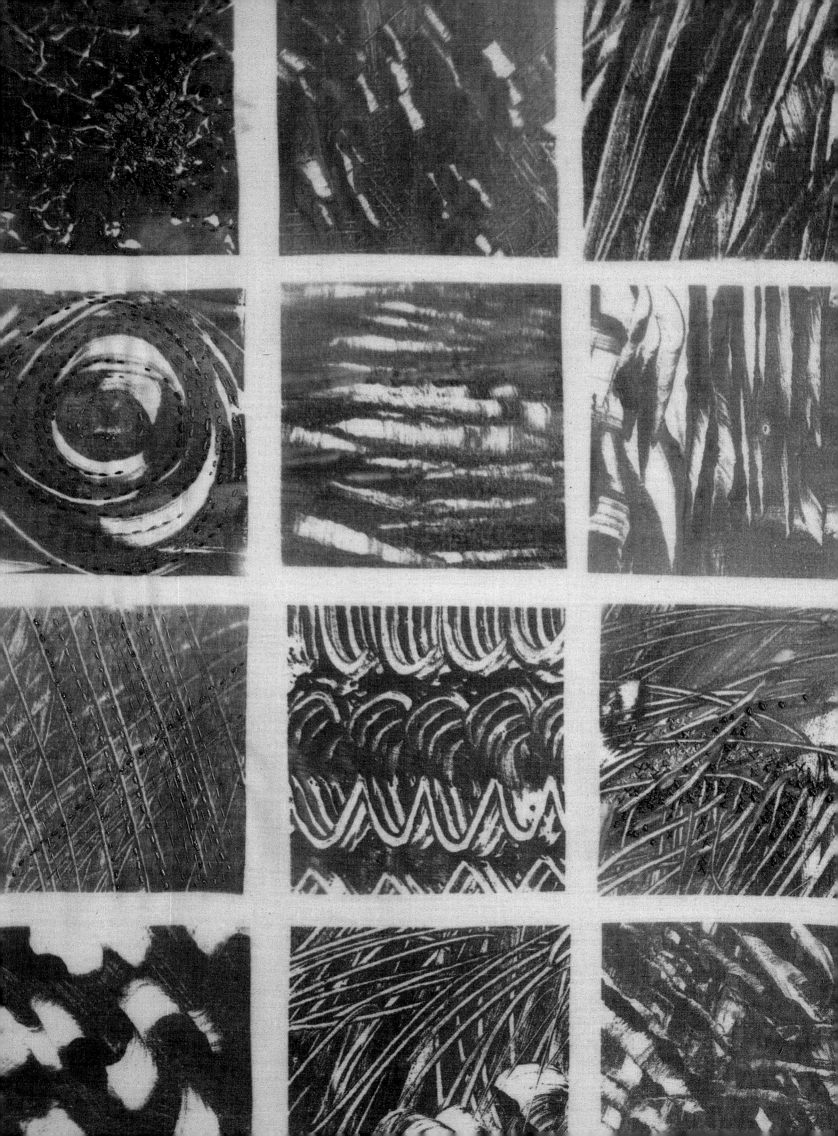

This section of a belt (right) *shows various materials, including velvets which have been layered, transfer printed, partially cut back and machine embroidered. Straight, zigzag, cable stitches and machine-made cords have been used to emphasize the design. (Mary Way)*

Transfer paints (far right) *were printed onto a synthetic velvet layered with semi-transparent and metallic fabrics and then decorated with automatic stitch patterns. (Joan McQuillan)*

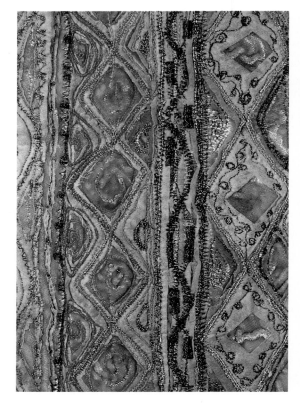 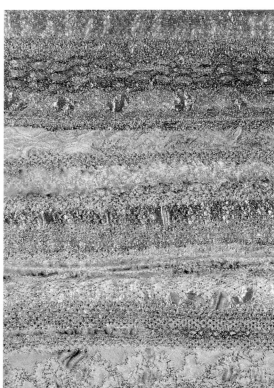

This interesting range of work (right) *was inspired by the studies of tattoos and body painting. Experiments were worked with transfer paints, wax resist, masking fluid, cut-back appliqué and machine embroidery. (Clémence Gilder)*

Patterns (opposite page) *were transfer painted and printed onto a synthetic fabric. Small pieces were cut up and applied to the background with metallic machine threads. Notice how the densely worked machine stitches incorporate and link the shapes. (Lizzie Ettinger)*

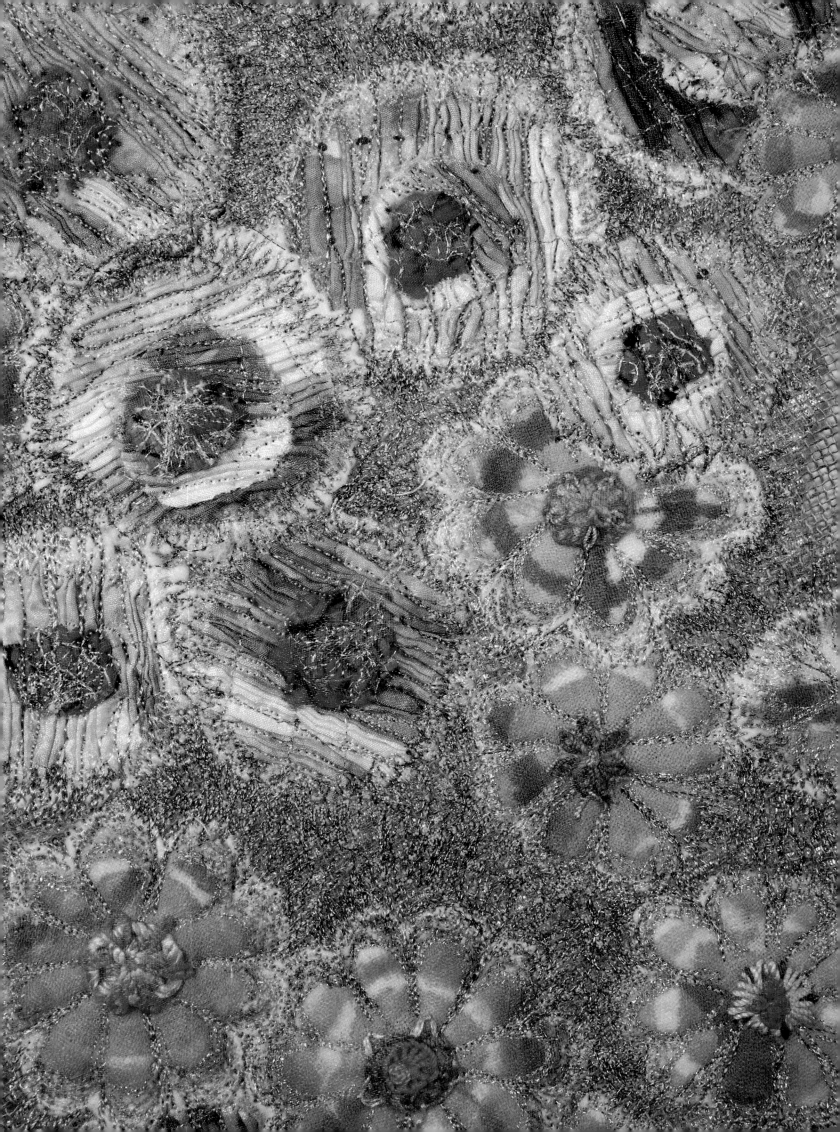

SILK PAINTS

These versatile paints can be used to colour most fabrics. They are non-toxic, water-soluble and can be fixed by ironing.

Protect your work surface with newspaper, polythene sheeting or lining paper. Stretch the fabric on top and fix in place with small strips of masking tape. Alternatively you can stretch, pin or staple the fabric over a wooden frame. Ensure that all materials have been washed to clear any 'dressing' and ironed to eradicate any creasing which might effect the evenness of the colour to be applied.

Paint can be mixed in a plate to make the required colour adding white for pastel shades and more water for paler tints. The paint can be applied by brush or sponge. The fluid consistency of the paint means that the colours will gradually merge and combine to make a third. Although any fabric can be used, the paint flows best on silk or silky type cloth. An easier flow of paint is achieved by slightly dampening the fabric with a sponge dipped in clear water, but of course this will also dilute the colour a little. Wonderful colour effects can be created and will provide inspiring backcloths for your stitching. Do remember to work quite quickly as 'tide marks' can occur. Applying paint onto fabric stretched tautly over a frame helps to eliminate this problem. However, these marks can sometimes be used creatively as guidelines for hand or machine stitching.

For a variety of effects, try the following:
1. Apply the silk paint to a variety of fabrics and note the different reactions.
2. Apply the paint onto dry, slightly dampened and wet fabric.
3. Having sponged the silk paint onto the cloth, apply droplets of clear water after a few minutes. Interesting effects will be achieved by partially diluting the colour.
4. Place grains of rock, sea or dishwasher-machine salt on top of the wet paint.
5. Sponge or brush permanent or metallic paint onto the fabric. Immediately apply silk paint to flood in and around the shapes.
6. Mix a little pearl permanent paint with the silk paint for a slightly opaque, mother-of-pearl, effect.

Panel inspired by an area of medieval tiled flooring in Salisbury Cathedral. Handmade paper was applied to felt, which had been coloured with silk paints, and machine and hand stitched in silk threads. (Jenni Last)

GUTTA/RESIST

Gutta is a solution which is painted onto the cloth to act as a boundary preventing one colour from flowing into another. Clear, coloured and metallic gutta, or outliners, are available. If using coloured gutta allow for coloured lines in the design plan as only the clear solution washes out. Also, in order for the gutta to work properly, the fabric needs to be stretched tautly over a frame to prevent it from touching another surface and smudging.

To increase and develop your knowledge of the effects which can be achieved with clear gutta, attempt the following. Apply by using:
1. a plastic dispenser with a nozzle
2. a plastic dispenser with a fine nib attached
3. a fine brush (size 00,0,1)
4. any of the above but not a continuous line
5. a sponge, cork, string or other items.
Coloured or metallic outlines can be applied in exactly the same way.

Other trials could be made by diluting coloured guttas with clear, mixing clear gutta with silk paints, or by using permanent metallic paints as a resist to see how effective they are. Always be ready to experiment. Use up your fabric remnants for your trials and allow time to discover the boundaries of this particular medium. These sessions can often produce unusual patterns and effects.

When the silk paint is dry, remember to iron it to fix the colour. You will notice that the fabric will regain its softness once it has been pressed. Any remaining stiffness, caused by the gutta or excess paint, can be removed by washing in a gentle soap solution.

PERMANENT FABRIC PAINTS

Permanent, pearl and metallic fabric paints can also be used easily by applying them directly onto the fabric by brush or sponge. The thicker consistency of these paints allows definite marks and shapes to be retained. The paint can be diluted to give a colour wash effect if desired. Softer effects can be achieved by burnishing the edges of the painted shapes using a soft rag, or finger, to merge and blend the colour into the background. The pigment retained on the surface does impair the feel and quality of the cloth, giving it a stiffish feel which is not so comfortable to stitch into. However, the results can be stunning and you may consider such effects are necessary for your design needs and override any negative considerations.

Paper, card, adhesive, clear film and masking tape can also be used as design aids with this paint. You can find further useful information in *The Art of the Needle* (see page 141).

Many people like the finer qualities achieved by applying fabric paint with an airbrush and at least two manufacturers now produce fabric colours designed for this purpose. Looking through specialist magazines, suppliers' catalogues and visiting some trade fairs should keep you informed about new products coming onto the market (see page 142).

Outline patterns (opposite, above) *were painted in various gutta colours. Silk paint was flooded into the spaces. The designs were inspired by studying patterns from other cultures* (see pages 62 and 63) *(Willemien Stevens)*

This section (opposite, below), *taken from a cumberband, shows metallic-gold permanent paint printed onto dyed shot silk. Machine embroidery and beads have been incorporated to create a rich surface. (Mary Way)*

Rock, sea, dishwasher salt and droplets of clear water were applied to create this special effect on Silk Habotai (below) *which had just been coloured with Deka silk paints* (see page 142). *(Jane E. Clarke)*

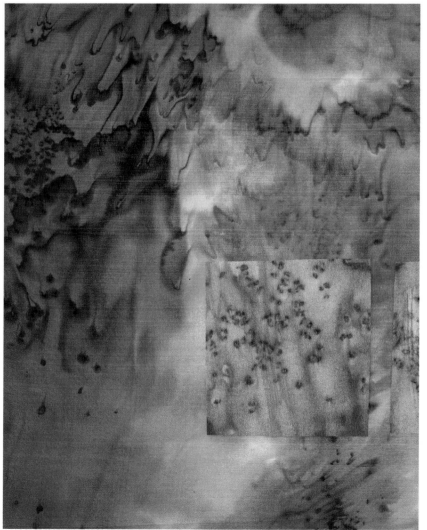

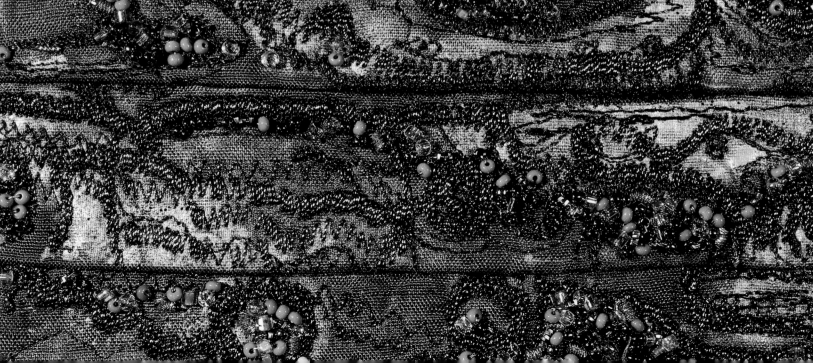

REDISCOVERING APPLIQUE

It is always very satisfying to colour background fabrics in a variety of ways and to create wonderful schemes and patterns which are unique to you. The difficulty comes in trying to develop these surfaces. The particular effect you have achieved may be suitable for hand or machine quilting, or to be pieced into a patchwork or decorated further with surface stitchery. Alternatively you may wish to build up and enrich the cloth by applying more materials. These may also have been coloured with fabric paints or purchased already coloured. A combination of both can work but do be aware that sometimes the evenly coloured commercial fabrics can override the subtleties of those you have coloured yourself. Obviously, successful appliqué designs can be worked solely in these materials. The final surface could be made up from layers of sheers, their hues influenced by the 'underpainting' of the original ground material, or opaque fabrics which could be cut back to expose layers beneath. There are two main factors to be borne in mind. Firstly, the fabric to be applied should be sympathetic to the background. Secondly, the choice of edging and the method of sewing down should be appropriate and sensitively incorporated (or considered) within the context of the design. If the appliqué is to be functional similar types of fabrics should be chosen to ensure compatibility for cleaning purposes.

To eliminate puckering it is advisable for the warp and weft of the fabric to be applied to line up with that of the base cloth. There are always exceptions to the rule and deliberate fraying or 'shot' qualities may need to be exaggerated as part of the design. It is generally best to select a thread the colour of the fabric to be applied for sewing down purposes so that the stitches do not compete with any decorative stitching. However a freer type of appliqué may include stitches that have a multipurpose role; to hold the fabric in place as well as being a part of the textural surface.

Rust Fragment: *Polycotton was printed with transfer paint which had first been sponged onto paper. Layers of sheer fabric, thread snippets and nets were burnt, distressed and bonded on the background fabric. Machine stitches including satin stitch beading and cable stitch were worked in metallic yarns. Hand stitching including straight, seeding and french knot stitches were added for textural effect.*

BONDING PAPER

Bonding paper (transfer fusing web) is coated with a fine film of adhesive and as a means of applying one fabric to another has a great number of advantages. Ironing the rough (adhesive) side of the paper onto the back of the fabric to be applied stiffens it which makes it extremely easy to cut out intricate shapes. Once this has been completed, peel the backing paper away and place the fabric, sticky side down on the background, cover with a dampened cloth and iron to bond the shape in place. The resulting appliqué does not affect the feel of the fabric more than any other method but, more importantly, it lies very flat easing the process of hand or machine stitching the edge, if required, and totally eliminating the need for preliminary pinning and tacking. However, additional layers will eventually result in the material stiffening and stitching into it will not be easy. Hand stitching may not be so pleasurable and machine needles will blunt quickly. Although the advantages outweigh the disadvantages it must be said that some of you will still prefer the gentle undulations of traditional appliqué.

Freer unusual effects can be created by using the bonding paper in an unconventional way. By tearing the paper, an edge of thin adhesive film will be exposed. Separate it from the backing paper, taking care not to lose it as it seems to have a life of its own. Any draught caused by laughing, sneezing or even from the heat of an iron seems to make it magically disappear. It is

Cloth coloured with silk paints was bonded to a natural calico background before being sewn in place by machined zigzag stitches in toning threads. The simple design for this cushion (above) *was inspired by tile patterns from Crete. The slightly uneven colours found within the tiles were reflected in the application of silk paint.*

SEWING DOWN

Appliqué for functional embroidery should be sewn in place as firmly as possible to withstand wear and tear. For heavy duty use, a machined close satin stitch would be advisable. Close zigzag stitch opened out just a little secures the edge but has a slightly softer look.

For those of you who prefer not to use a machine, there are some effective hand-sewn methods. Herringbone and buttonhole stitches are the usual ones to choose. All the methods described so far result in a comparatively flat and smooth surface. For a very neat edge which is slightly raised, blind or hemmed appliqué may be your choice. The edges of the pieces to be applied are turned under and slip stitched into place. Allow extra fabric for the turnings when cutting out.

Non-fraying fabrics such as felt or leather can be slip stitched or saddle stitched in place. Net or tulle can be attached with tiny stitches worked over a bar of thread inside the cut edge.

Fabric paints were airbrushed onto the background and fabric shapes bonded on top (left). *Layers of polyester wadding were placed under the top material and machine stitches worked to emphasize the main shapes resulting in a quilted surface. (Peggy Crowley)*

a good idea to weight it down in one particular place on your work surface or actually pin it to your clothes.

Tear the adhesive film into tiny pieces and place them on the background cloth within the particular area of your design. Snip scraps of fabric or thread on top of the film using tweezers, if necessary, to position these delicate fragments. Some of you may get carried away with enthusiasm so if too thick a layer builds up place more pieces of the bonding material on top. Position a pale coloured sheer fabric such as a cheap chiffon scarf over the areas being built up To protect the chiffon place a sheet of baking parchment (silicone paper) on top and iron to bond all the layers together. The chiffon should not alter the general colour too much and helps to sandwich everything together. The iron should be hot enough to fuse the layers together and melt away the adhesive without burning or melting any synthetic top fabric. This unusual surface can then be further embellished with all sorts of stitched decoration as well as being incorporated within an appliqué. Although some of these creative surfaces can be used as a top fabric intricate bonded pieces could look most effective if topped with another such as felt, parts of which could be then cut back to expose exotic or intriguing patches of texture.

This waistcoat (opposite page) *was made from a richly decorated fabric which was made by integrating and bonding snippets of fabric, thread and paillettes within a 'sandwich' of chiffon and silk. Additional texture was achieved by straight stitches worked on top. (Margaret Jones)*

dering iron and to work on an old tin tray, or something similar, as a work surface. Soldering iron sets are now available with a choice of ends enabling you to make a selection of fine, broad and decorative marks. Only time will tell if the tiny carbon deposits from the burning processes will perish the cloth but as this appliqué is usually used with top stitching, any tendency to perish would be hardly noticeable.

A more textural form of appliqué can be achieved by trapping small fragments of cloth in all over machine stitches. Alternatively a subtle, integrated surface can be built up by placing fabric shapes onto a background and darning the ground cloth partially into and around the appliqué. Unless deliberately choosing a holding down stitch to highlight or add further pattern to the design, select stitches which will enhance it, for example, freely worked cross, Cretan or straight stitch variations would be very effective.

Small, frayed cloth pieces bonded and machined in place were used to create this distinctive waistcoat (opposite page). (Anna Johnson)

This interesting surface (left) shows a section of an old wall in Crete.

This sample (below) shows a range of fabrics which sport a variety of edgings and stitches.

CHOOSING THE EDGES

Having revised the basic method of appliqué the fun really starts when freer interpretative or patterned imagery is sought. Look at your sketches, reference photos and designs to help you decide how you wish to interpret them in appliqué. Ask yourself the following questions. What type of edges are contained within it? Are they crisp, precise, or do they blend in? Are they eroded or do they stand slightly proud? Having made your assessment select a suitable method of applying the various cloth shapes. Depending on the desired effect, you may wish to cut the fabric out, turn it under and slip stitch precisely or roll the edges to suggest a raised border or gentle ridge. An irregular edge could be torn, frayed, ripped, cut, distressed, unevenly cut, burnt in parts, or singed to fuse the edge to prevent fraying.

However, do beware as burnt edges can be gimmicky if used indiscriminately but can look absolutely stunning if used appropriately. When deliberately burning or scorching to achieve a certain effect take care to follow a few safety rules. Ensure that your workspace is well ventilated as some fabrics give off toxic fumes. Never attempt to use a candle. It is dangerous as you have so little control. A match is easier to use but have a bowl of water close by in case of accidental flare ups. The best method is to use a sol-

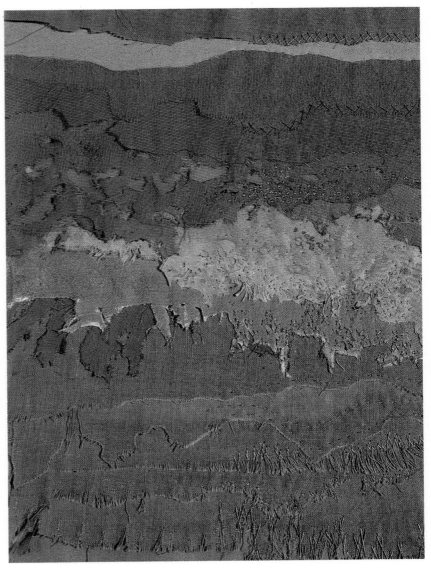

Various fabrics (right) *including sheers, printed tissue, Vilene and chiffons were applied, machine embroidered and partially cut back. Some sections were trapped within a grid of machine-stitched squares and cords. (Linda M. Scott)*

Appliqué showing layers of sheer and semi-transparent fabrics (below). *The top layer is transfer printed and decorated with machine-embroidered, running and tufting stitches. (Linda M. Scott)*

APPLIED LAYERS

Spectacular surfaces can be achieved by layering a range of fabrics, partly stitching them together and then cutting or slashing through the layers to expose the colours beneath. Machine stitching provides a firm stitch enabling the fabric to be cut away close to the stitched line. For decorative, non-functional work these cut edges will only tend to fray back to the machining. Felt is a pleasing fabric to work with and can be cut back with no fear of fraying. Consider whether to soften the precise edge.

Be adventurous and try appliqué methods new to you. Cloth fragments can be applied to soluble fabrics and machine stitches worked incorporating the applied shapes and contrasting them with lacy inserts. On completion some of the new pieces could be applied to form a flat surface whilst others could be manipulated into raised areas.

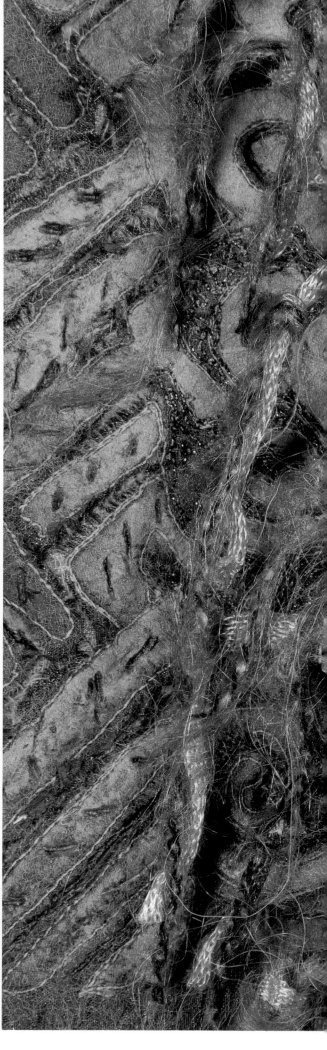

MANIPULATING FABRICS

Attractive textural surfaces can be created with fabric and then pieced and patched together or applied to a background cloth. Initially, you will need to know how certain fabrics react and how to exploit their qualities. Materials containing natural fibres tend to crease more readily, a disadvantage if you wish to wear the fabric but a definite advantage for creating pin tucks or assembling patchwork. Synthetic fibres are less crushable and more springy to work with. Other fabrics stretch, contain heavy slubbed yarns within their weave or easily fray and disintegrate when cut into tiny pieces.

Acquaint yourself with the creative capabilities of a range of fabrics by working through some of the following suggestions.

Firstly, select four or five materials to include a sheer, perhaps chiffon or organza, a medium weight such as cotton or calico and a thicker, coarser cloth such as denim or tweed. A synthetic and natural fibre could also be included. Cut each cloth into smaller pieces to enable you to attempt the following.

• Distress the cloth by pulling it out of shape and fraying the edges

• Attempt to make a hole in it by:
1. rearranging the threads and 'pulling' a hole
2. piercing it with a stiletto, scissors or knitting needle
3. cutting away a section of cloth to:
    – distress, fray and pull it out of shape
    – push other fabrics and threads up through the hole
• Gathering, ruching and quilting the material
• Folding it in pleats, tucks and smocking
• Cutting, slashing and burning the cloth. Note what happens to the edges. Do they disintegrate, fray badly, curl or bubble up?
• Can you reassemble or piece it together by:
1. machining the cloth on soluble fabrics
2. freely working insertion stitches (using stiff paper as the initial backing)
3. overlaying and overlapping the fabric in regular or haphazard arrangements
• Do small lengths of the cloth roll, scrunch up or manipulate suitably for small padded patches?
• Do longer lengths, cut on the bias, make successful rouleaus or yarns to stitch with?
• How do the various fabric paints react to each type of cloth?

Experimenting with a vast range of fabrics including 'shots', velvets, metallic, embossed and non-fraying felts and leathers could provide a creative challenge for a long period of time.

Soft, finely woven calico (left) was cut into strips, woven, knotted, plaited, twisted and couched in place to form an interesting surface. (Louise Ellis)

Handmade felt (opposite page) was layered and partially cut back to expose areas of sumptuous textural hand and machine stitchery. (Gwen Hedley)

Strips of paper and cloth (below) were twisted, knotted and manipulated to form a grid arrangement which was then decorated with stitchery. (Gwen Hedley)

STITCH THEMES

You may already practise certain embroidery skills which do not necessarily involve creative hand stitching, perhaps patchwork, quilting or machine embroidery. This section could help you to rediscover the joys, scope and creativity of decorative surface stitches. Some of the following suggestions will expand the range of patterned, textured and coloured effects which can be achieved.

Initially consider your purpose for choosing to stitch. If your planned project is to be functional, washed or worn, there would obviously be certain restrictions on your choice of thread and fabric, and you would have to take into account the suitability of the chosen stitched surface. Alternatively if experimental samples or decorative pieces are to be tackled, exciting lateral thinking can be applied.

There are only a few ground rules. The background fabric should be selected bearing in mind the weight of the thread to be worked. However, this problem can often be overcome by placing a thinner cloth, such as printed polycotton on top of a firmer one such as calico or a piece of old sheeting. The threads to be worked should also be compatible with the ground cloth. A much wider choice of threads than imagined can be used but obviously if during the stitching process the size of the yarn tears or puckers the cloth too much then that particular combination may well be wrong.

If you have collected a range of interesting commercial or home-dyed yarns, allow yourself time to 'play' or experiment using a range of stitches on different fabric backgrounds. These samples could then act as a type of stitch dictionary and will help you to select the right effect for a particular interpretation. Rather than always attempting a finished project, stitch small areas of colour and texture possibly using your fabric paint trials for backgrounds. The new effects learnt will certainly help you to go on and create some original and pleasing images.

Eugenia's Lemon Tree (100cm x 100cm) by Audrey Walker. Layers of machine stitchery were developed further by the addition of many hand stitches resulting in this highly decorative surface. (Photograph by Annie Morris)

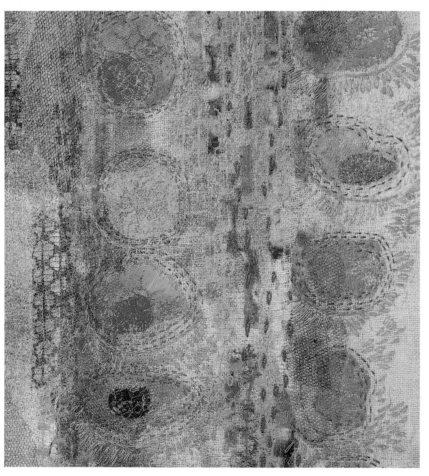

LINE STITCHES

If you are about to explore the exciting world of hand embroidery or are looking to follow new avenues, it is worth equipping yourself with the knowledge of just a few stitches. One or two plus their variations will be more than adequate to achieve rich surfaces. Too often skilled needlewomen feel that they must include a wide range and in doing so lose the overall unity of the design often resulting in a 'busy' disjointed look with one stitch competing with, rather than enhancing another.

Learn a few line stitches such as couching, double knot or one of the chain stitch family. Using these stitches to 'draw' you can outline or depict an image or place them closely together to form a solid stitched surface perhaps indicating the spaces around or between the chosen shapes. Flowing, linear or solid areas can be stitched quite accurately depending on the yarn used. Torn, fraying fabric strips would give a more textural result whereas a round, smooth shiny thread would show the stitch more clearly defined. You will find that such factors will influence your choice when striving to interpret a particular object or surface.

TEXTURAL STITCHING

Areas or drifts of textural stitches can contrast and complement the linear or plain sections of your design. There are many to choose from including seeding, detached chain, french and bullion knots.

DETACHED CHAIN

Detached chain or 'lazy daisy' is a much maligned stitch because of its association with rather mundane transfer embroidery sometimes featured in popular women's magazines. Try some of the following suggestions.
1. Vary the thickness of thread. One strand or a very fine yarn gives a straight stitch look whereas a thicker wool gives a chunkier result.
2. Try working the stitch with unusual yarns such as ribbons, or strips cut from tights.
3. Taking up a larger piece of the ground fabric in the stitch process will look like a leaf shape whereas a tiny fragment of cloth picked up will appear as a rounder mark.
4. Groups of similar length stitches can be worked in blocks with others worked on top at right angles to the first. Layering two stitches on top of two others produces a 'dot' effect providing an alternative to the french knot.
5. This stitch looks extremely attractive when

placed in a random haphazard arrangement and can appear as a bulkier version of seeding.
6. Vary the tension. A loose stitch will appear more looped, a tight one as a dot or a knot.

SEEDING

Seeding is a random, haphazard arrangement of tiny running stitches. This version of straight stitch is extremely useful for helping to blend shapes into a background. It can also be worked in toning colours to texture a backcloth, adding another dimension, without intruding on the main design features. Use a variety of threads and allow some stitches to encroach or be worked on top of the others. Too much space between can give a 'spotty' uncoordinated effect. For a rich, raised surface wrap another yarn several times over the bar of the stitch. Multicoloured or metallic thread could look particularly attractive.

FRENCH KNOTS

This extremely popular stitch is a joy to work although time consuming if worked in concentrated areas. The conventional method is to twist the thread twice around the needle. For a neat, round knot pull the thread tightly at this stage before continuing to take the needle to the back of the fabric, almost at the same point as the thread first emerged. An even tighter knot will form if the thread is twisted only once around the needle.

Other textural effects can be achieved by experimenting. On twisting and tightening the thread around the needle, pull the thread only partially through to the back leaving a small loop. Hold the loop until you have worked the next knot which will secure it. The characteristics of each thread whether soft, fine, or stiff, will determine the final result.

Another variation is to work the stitch accurately until the thread is taken to the back of the cloth. Then, instead of inserting the needle close to where it first emerged, place it a little distance away and knots with little 'legs' will be formed. Incorporating beads into the work process is another consideration.

These three stitches have been featured many times before and remain universally popular. Perhaps you could consider finding alternative textural 'dots' and 'blobs' by using a new range of stitches. Some of them are traditionally used as line stitches but worked as single units can create rich surfaces. Raised chain band, knotted cable chain, rosette chain or double knot stitches could all be given a trial run. The examples shown are most inspirational.

Having practised small groups of stitches ask yourself the following questions:
● Did you try a variety of threads contrasting matt and shiny, smooth and twisted or fraying strips?
● Did you vary the scale and tension to achieve large, small, tight or loose forms?
● Did you work, blend in or merge the threads onto a dyed ground cloth, an appliqué pattern or onto machine embroidery?

Single double-knot stitches (left) *have been used to create an unusual texture combining a variety of matt and shiny threads. (Carolyn Walker)*
Wax resist and silk fabric paints (below) *were used to colour the slubbed background cloth. French knots were then worked in silk and metallic thread. (Anne Jones)*
Sheer fabrics and nets (opposite top) *which had been coloured with fabric paints were applied and bonded to form a new fabric. (Mary Way)*
This beautiful hat (opposite below) *is made of silk which has been coloured with silk and transfer paints. Single knotted cable chain stitches have been used to create this rich decorative surface. (Carolyn Walker)*

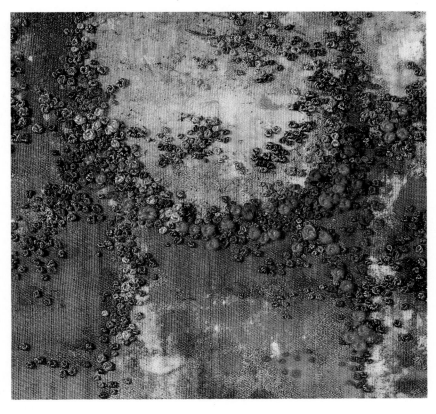

The knowledge learned from these stitch trials will help you interpret observed surfaces when taken out of context. Look in your garden, a local park or nearby buildings and see if you can find small areas or patterns which could be interpreted in french knots, single double-knot stitch or a combination of several. The ridges of worm casts in damp sand, glistening droplets of water, the subtle colours and indentations of a sea urchin or seams of glittering quartz within a rock formation could all be inspiring starting points for textural adventures.

LAYERS

Many stitches can be worked in a variety of ways to form all over textural surfaces ranging from ridges, holes and lacy knotted tracery through to chunky lumps and bumps.

Raised chain band stitch is one of the best loved and most versatile of stitches. It can be used as a line stitch, as single units or as a filling stitch. It can be partially layered to expose other colours or textures beneath, darned and woven with fabric strips or ribbons, or used with beads, bonded pieces or wrapped threads.

The buttonhole stitch family offers another attractive alternative. Looped, knotted or detached buttonhole can be stitched across part of the design. Many differing effects will be achieved by varying the thread, spacing and tension of the stitch. The initial stitches can act as support for further layers to be built on. The loopy quality of this stitch could give the ideal foundation for weaving, darning, machine lace

insertions or for hanging tassels and beads. Buttonhole picots can be haphazardly stitched to a certain length and then manipulated, twisted, rolled, scrunched or ruched and sewn in place to create a rich, knobbly, encrusted surface. Combined with fabric strips or beads will give it yet another dimension. Strips of fabric, machined cords or coils of threads held down by any of these stitches offer further avenues of exploration.

The following words may help you to be inventive and to explore these stitches further and not be timid in your trials. Layers, ridges, crevices, indentations, erosions, craters could help you to select surfaces with these characteristics enabling you to look, draw, and photograph from everyday life or research from books or museums. Gnarled or blasted trees, surfaces partially eaten by insects, wasps nests or the scales and lumps found on many reptiles could form the basis of some natural design sources. Alternatively man-made items such as wood carvings, stoneware urns, embossed metal or intricate jewellery may interest you more. Interpreting these surfaces through stitched textiles will offer you new and unique qualities to enjoy.

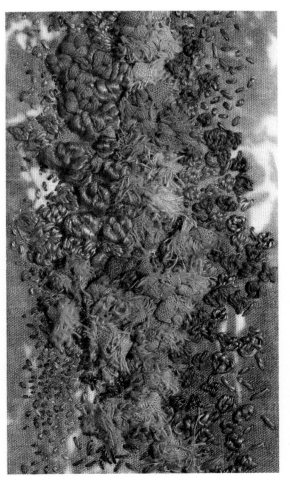

Variations of knotted buttonhole and beadwork on transfer-coloured polycotton and Vilene (left). *(Reni Tajima)*

Single raised chain band stitch (left) *worked in silk, wool and knitting tape on fabric which was coloured by printing from crumpled paper sponged with transfer paint.*

Crumbling walls inspired this textural piece (opposite page). *Dyed background materials were built up with appliqué, french knots and seeding worked in a wide variety of threads* (see page 42). *(Clémence Gilder)*

107

*These photographs
(right) provided the
starting points for the
accompanying sketches.
Movement lines were
traced for design
purposes in order to
select and exaggerate
certain features.*

WORDS AND MOVEMENT

The qualities created by a stitched surface are amazingly varied. Being aware of how to show movement within a design can lead you down new avenues and in some instances give additional verve to your embroidery.

Initially select some words which suggest movement. These could include:

meander	waving	staccato
flow	undulate	counter rhythm
whizz	spin	rhythm
whirl	disintegrate	crisscross
swirl	explode	growth.

Using a pen or pencil make doodles in your sketch book indicating marks that you think are characteristic of some of the words you have listed (see sketches opposite).

Progress to simple stitched marks on fabric. Variations of straight stitch such as satin, running, tacking or seeding could be useful. Line stitches, perhaps couching, twisted chain or coral stitches offer another choice. Cretan, herringbone or fly stitches all have their unique look and conventional usage but by taking new directions and initiatives new patterns and styles could evolve. The use of colour can also emphasize particular elements. Remember that in general, warm colours come to the fore and cool ones retreat into the background.

Having experienced this particular approach, develop these ideas further by working the same exercises on top of printed and coloured fabrics. Taking rubbings from card or PVA blocks (see pages 80 and 81), or found surfaces, could help accentuate patterns with colour and the textural marks could possibly suggest the

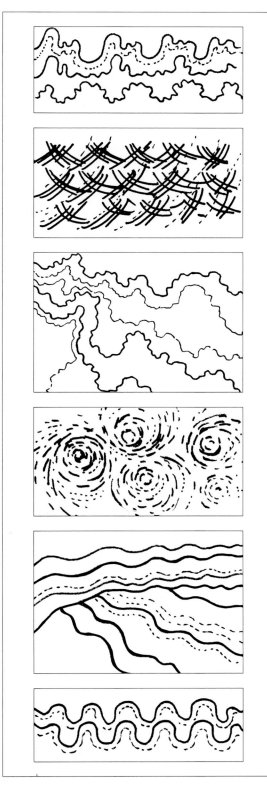

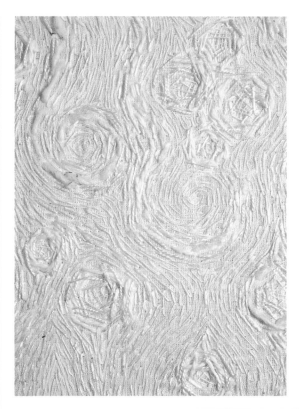

A wonderful sense of movement (left) *has been achieved by working straight stitches in a variety of matt and shiny yarns. (Lee Foreman)*

This sensitively coloured appliqué (below) *has been decorated with twisted chain stitches to suggest gentle movement. (Reni Tajima)*

type of stitch to select for enhancing the design.

To develop these ideas further interpret some of your written observations or select some descriptive passages from poetry or prose. These could be most inspiring and help you to select certain colours, threads and appropriate stitches.

TONES

The example below demonstrates how tone can be shown by intensifying the fabric paint colours and hand stitching. (Liz Harding)

As indicated earlier, stitches can be interpreted in a linear or textural way and be perfectly adequate and interesting just in their own right. They can also be organized tonally so that form and distance within a design can be indicated if desired.

To acquaint yourself with tonal qualities study the drawings of famous artists such as Rembrandt, Picasso, Henry Moore or David Hockney. Observe, write notes and make quick sketches of sections of their work. Note the method of mark-making whether pen, pencil,

ink and wash, crayon or charcoal. Take isolated sections out of context and look at the way the artist has indicated shadows, form and texture on a surface. Identify the main type of mark that forms the basis of the shading. They could include diagonal lines, dots, squiggles, cross-hatching, or short directional strokes. Jot down small sets of marks. This is a marvellous way of getting to know the different styles as well as helping you to appreciate each particular interpretation and the skills involved. Do not think that embroidery images should mimic these qualities exactly but the marks made with a range of drawing media have certain qualities

which could be quite easily translated into creative stitchery. There is much to be learnt from other disciplines.

Select some sections from your jottings to interpret in stitch, experimenting with at least two stitches to see if you can obtain similar effects. Keep these samples for future reference.

Dots and dashes could be interpreted using knots and detached chain stitch; lines and squiggles in couching or chain stitch and variations of crosshatching in cross stitch and straight stitch. Refer to your own stitch reference to help you select other appropriate stitches.

This particular exercise will help familiarize you with the closeness or sparsity of certain marks and the experience gained will provide a good foundation for the next suggestion.

Cut a strip of plain white thin card or paper and fold, bend or curve it into a simple shape. Place it in front of you, taking care to light it in one direction only so you are not confused with a multiplicity of shadows. Note where and when the tones vary from light to dark taking special note of the exact shape of the dark areas and cast shadows. Drawing these areas correctly will help to indicate the fullness, form or three-dimensional quality of the paper shape. On completion select a small section and, taking it out of context, make a stitch interpretation referring back to your stitch experiments.

Similar exercises could follow which would be most beneficial for your powers of observation and improve your drawing skills. Objects to experiment with could include a cylinder, a sphere (such as an apple or orange), a section of a tree or hilly landscape, a face, or sections of buildings.

The following suggestions will help you achieve certain effects and carrying out these small exercises would be useful experience
• Using the same stitch and thread vary the spacing working sparsely then densely.
• Using the same colour and stitch, vary the thickness of the thread.
• Vary the tones of one colour from its lightest to darkest shade.
• Change the size of the stitch, its density, spacing and colour tones to combine all the above suggestions.

To summarize, form and distance within stitching can be achieved by using a range of tones within a colour scheme, by contrasting the density, sparseness or spacing of the stitch, by the use of thick, thin, fine or heavy thread as well as indicating the movement and direction of the main design shapes. Finally the textural

quality of the chosen yarn should reflect not only the surface to be interpreted but how effective it can be in helping to create the feeling of form. Matt surfaces tend to retreat and merge into the background whereas a shiny one will reflect the light and feature more prominently.

Examples of some typical types of shading (above). *From left to right: Henry Moore, David Hockney, Rembrandt.*

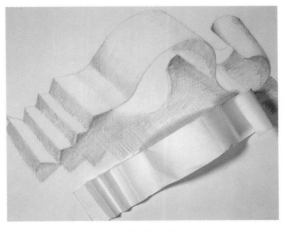

This picture (left) *shows the folded and curved piece of paper alongside the pencil drawing which inspired the accompanying stitched sample* (below). *(Ann V. Sutton)*

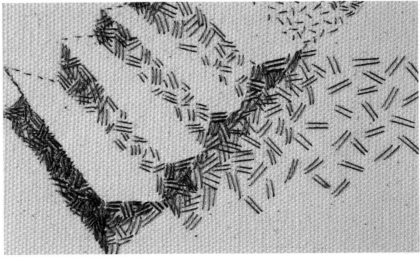

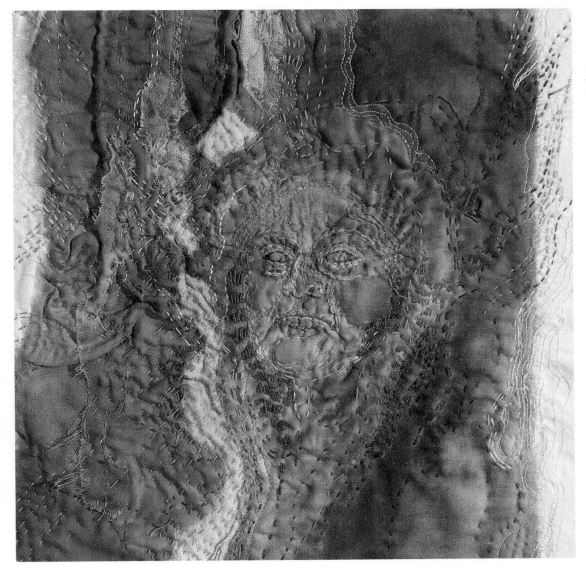

The colour scheme for this sumptuous piece (opposite page) *was inspired by the iridescent feathers of a golden pheasant. Threads, fabric and raffia were bonded onto silk which had been painted with transfer, silk and metallic fabric paints. Machine-wrapped cords, yarns and gold threads were couched or stitched over and through the applied shapes, linking and integrating them into a coherent whole. (Anne Jones)*

Three layers of lightweight polycotton (left) *were embellished with running stitches in the style of Bengali Kanthas. To help blend the imagery, silk paint was applied over the base stitching, along with further hand and machine stitchery. (Liz Harding)*

LINKING SHAPES

Stitches can be instrumental in relating, linking or unifying shapes within a design as often the motifs are totally unrelated to one another. This can be partially rectified by colour used sympathetically to link the design to its background but selecting the appropriate stitching provides that essential finishing touch. It can integrate all the various elements and prevent the isolated shapes looking as if they had been imposed on the background.

Before embarking on a large project allow time for trials. Make quick sketches of groups of circles, squares, or rectangles. Photocopy them to give a number of prints. Draw continuous lines emphasizing or going across the shapes in as many arrangements as possible. Using new photocopies of the same patterns sketch broken, directional or diagonal lines and dots around, through or across the shapes. Vary the thickness of the single mark as well as the density of multiples of marks. Rubbings or prints could prove to be quick methods of placing a coloured image on fabric. Follow this procedure by working a variety of simple stitches to link, blend, merge, trail, accentuate, outline or blur within, across or around the main patterns to unite the whole design within a given shape.

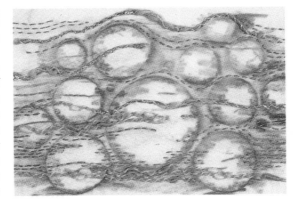

This rubbing (left), *taken from cardboard shapes using transfer crayons, was printed onto fabric. The shapes were linked with couched thread and running stitches. (Wendy Lowes)*

113

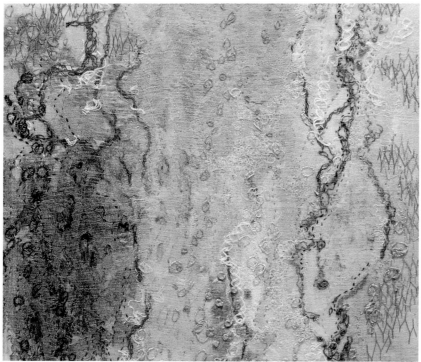

STITCH INTERPRETATIONS

Interpreting the decorative surfaces and patterns which can be found all around us is another direction many people look to for inspiration. A number of suggestions have already been made in *Book I – Design to Embroider* on how to look for and select designs which can then be developed through paper studies into fabric and thread images. However some of you may like to begin making your observations and first drawings very simply. The following considerations would apply to all sorts of topics but crops and fields have been selected in this instance. Those of you who do not feel too confident when jotting down ideas should begin by making an extremely quick diagram of a chosen section of farmland.

1. Limit your time – only spend 2-3 minutes on your sketch.

2. Before making a pencil mark on the paper, look at the forms in front of you and trace the shapes in the air with your fingers. This action simplifies the shape as your movement is too broad to allow for details. For instance if your hand was tracing a hedgerow it might follow the gently undulating bushes, make strong vertical strokes with a few twiddles for a line of poplar trees, continue with angular strokes for the roof of a barn, or trace the gently swaying partially vertical ears of corn. Having experienced this, quickly jot down on paper the simple marks you indicated in the air.

3. Always accompany the diagrams with notes such as those shown below:

> colours – type of green – silvery green/new fresh green/grey-purple green
>
> textures – quick darting movements of little leaves or crumbling soil with lots of stones proportions – broad indication of width of hedgerow compared to the field and sky.

Do not worry about perspective at this stage just keep to horizontal or vertical patterns.

For more information make other quick observations, both visually and verbally.

In general does the whole view seem to show

Hedgerow Arches (above left) *was created by painting and printing transfer fabric paint onto polycotton. Cretan and straight stitches worked in a range of toning colours were built up to create an effective image. (Christine Sheridan)*

Layers of semi-transparent fabrics (left) *were placed on a background cloth which had been transfer printed with an image. Detached chain, couching, Cretan and running stitches were added to accentuate certain design lines and textures. (Diane Senior)*

curvy indented lines against the sky with fields, or 'dotty' shapes in the foreground, or is the view flat and bleak with straight ridges?

What are the main characteristic growth patterns of the crops? Is the foreground full of short sharp vertical lines which might indicate stubble, or little frilly mounds of lettuce or vertical lines bent over at the top representing a field of leeks.

Remember you are gathering information in order to help you make a design. It is always better if this is based on observations but do not try to be too literal or photographic. Exaggerate or understate what you wish. Be inspired by the pattern, colour or texture and allow the unique characteristics of the fabrics and threads to shine through.

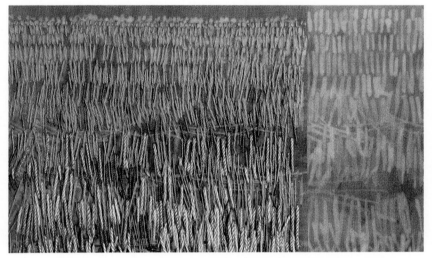

Quick two-minute sketches (above) *drawn by Pam Forbes (vegetables) and Fay Green (fields).*

This field of stubble (above right) *was the source of inspiration for the fabric and stitch design* (middle).

This interpretation of stubble (middle) *was first painted onto paper with masking fluid before the transfer paint was applied. The design was transferred onto the material and straight stitches, worked in a variety of threads, were built up; matt threads were used in the distance with more lustrous yarns in the foreground.*

A moorland scene (right) *worked in Cretan stitch was inspired by the design on page 59. (Barbara A. Woolner)*

115

MACHINE EMBROIDERY

Machine embroidery is an extremely exciting technique. With a little practice superb effects can be achieved enhancing the quality of the cloth as well as providing a wonderful foil for further embellishment with hand stitching. Each new machine model offers improved facilities such as a wider swing action or a larger range of automatic stitch patterns.

This short section dealing with this technique is to encourage you to create background fabrics which will be suitable for your designs, to revitalize your approach to textural machined surfaces and to revise your awareness of the scope of machined cords. They give an interesting effect in their own right as well as being extremely useful as a finishing process for some items. There are many good, informative books on all aspects of machine embroidery, some of which are listed on page 141. A comprehensive section covering this technique was also included in *The Art of the Needle*.

To set your machine for free stitching, lower the feed dogs or cover with a plate and set the stitch length to 'O'. Adjustments to the tension may need to be made. It is advisable to follow the manufacturer's manual taking note that this type of work is often listed under 'darning' as embroidery stitches usually refer to the automatic set patterns. Replace the foot with a wide darner. These have much improved of late. The initial 'blind spot' has been eliminated by the introduction of a transparent plastic foot or metal ones with front openings. Unless you are experienced, or are using a stiff fabric, it is always wise to stretch your material very tautly in a frame which has been bound with tape to prevent slipping. Always remember to machine into the well of the frame, to lower the presser foot lever, and to pull the bobbin thread up through the cloth before commencing the stitching.

These attractive bags were designed and made by Claire Johnson. Coloured with silk fabric paint, wonderful quilted and machine textured surfaces were then built up. Delicate edgings made by machining on soluble fabrics were integrated within the design. Machined cords were used for straps as well as for additional decoration. Claire's sketch books illustrate her ability to create unusual patterns and textures.

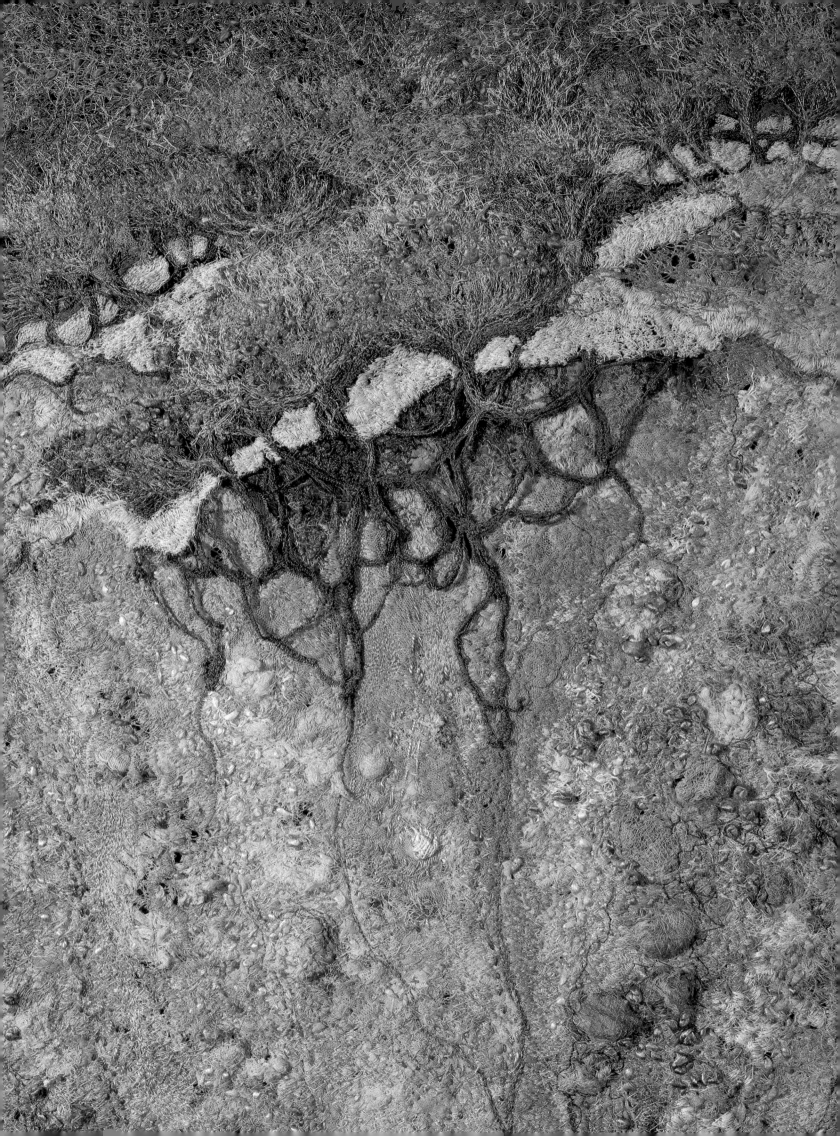

CREATING A BACKGROUND USING SOLUBLE FABRICS

Water-soluble fabrics offer new opportunities for creating totally new fabrics and providing non-fraying edges. The cold water type looks like thin plastic sheeting and tears easily. Use two or three layers in a frame and patch if splits occur during the work process. Once the stitching has been completed, dip it into a bowl of cold water to dissolve the fabric.

The boiling water-soluble fabrics look and feel more like conventional cloth. When you have finished the machining, use tongs to plunge it into boiling water to dissolve the ground fabric. Rinse in cold water. If there is any remaining sticky substance, dip the embroidery into the water again to clear. Do remember to link all the machined shapes together and to work the lines of the main structures several times, in order for the whole

A detail from View from the Cove *(opposite page): layers of machine embroidery and fabric pieces were applied to soluble fabric to create a new cloth. Machined cords and textural stitches have been incorporated in some areas. The design was based on observations of a Cretan coastline (page 137).*

piece to hold together, keep its shape and not disintegrate when the background is dissolved. Stretch the wet embroidery back to size and shape, pin to a board and leave to dry. Many dyed, bonded and machine-embroidered fabrics could be assembled and linked with lacy stitches, the whole piece could then be further embellished with more stitches, beads or other decorations. Each of these dissolving fabrics has its advantages and only experience with both will help you to chose which you prefer.

Another type of background can be made by machining a close grid of straight stitches on the boiling water-soluble fabric to form a sort of warp and weft. You can then build up the surface with solid areas of straight stitch, variations of zigzag and other textural effects. Tiny fragments of thread or fabric can be integrated as the stitched surface builds up. If larger holes are required for a certain design effect, the initial grid tracery can be snipped away after the dissolving process.

The examples shown in this section include a totally unique fabric made entirely of overlapping machine stitches, extremely attractive edgings and trims, small pieces applied and incorporated within a textural stitched surface, and, as a lacy pattern set into other materials. Strips of this machined fabric can also be rolled up to make attractive beads which can either be strung together to create textile jewellery or stitched onto a background cloth for a wonderfully rich effect.

A detail from Landscape within a Landscape *(above) showing machine-embroidered textural stitches worked on soluble fabric.*

The example (left) *shows the method of building a grid pattern in machined running stitches on soluble fabric. This is then covered with layers of zigzag stitch sometimes incorporating tiny fragments of cloth. Plunging the stitched piece, trimmed of any excess material, into boiling water eliminates the initial background material leaving a unique fabric made from a network of stitches.*

This unusual tree form (right) *was worked in solid machine-stitched pieces applied and padded to create a raised effect. (Judith Smalley)*

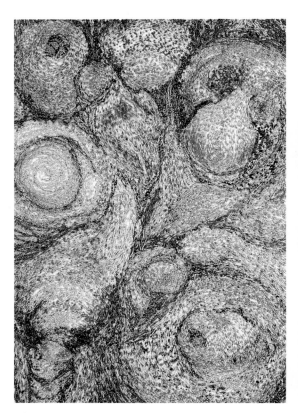

Handmade paper and gesso on organdy (far right) *which was coloured with silk and metallic fabric paints. The main textural effect was achieved by cable stitching on the machine. This sample was inspired by the design on page 45. (Louise Ellis)*

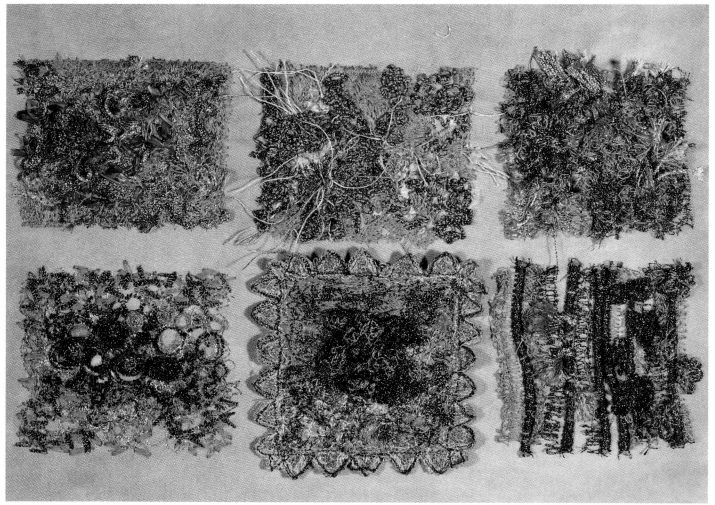

These exquisite gloves and bag (left) *were inspired by textural studies inspired by old walls (see page 51). They are made in dyed silk jersey and decorated with machine stitching on soluble fabrics incorporating french knots, seeding and beads. (Clémence Gilder)*

TEXTURAL SURFACES

It is always a good idea to revise your stitch vocabulary although time pressures often prevent you doing so. A new fabric, thread or an unusual combination of stitches can set you off down new creative paths. Try and evolve as many interesting machined surfaces as you can. List and work systematically through your ideas. Cable stitch, tufting or couching could all make challenging starting points. Some of the samples shown may remind you of the range of intriguing decorations which can be attained. You could quite possibly work at least six more samples in each technique by varying the colour combinations, the scale, the basic shapes, textural qualities or by incorporating other materials.

A set of intriguing textures created by machine stitches (opposite page).
Top row, from left to right: *a variety of yarns couched down by free running or zigzag stitches. Some areas have been accentuated by allowing loops to protrude.*
Zigzag stitches were worked over the surface and topped with layers of cable stitch. Fragments of fraying fabrics were incorporated.
Fringing textures created by looping threads over a card frame, machining down the centre line and cutting the loops on either side to enable the card to be retrieved.
Bottom row, from left to right: *the centre panel of this design was stitched with whip stitch and the edges in layers of satin stitched beading. Circles stitched in soluble fabric were applied to add a raised effect.*
Machine stitchery on soluble fabric making a new surface with a pretty non-fraying edge. Raised areas have been developed by applying beads which were made from strips of machine lace rolled and sewn in place.
Machine-stitched cords and zigzag stitches make a linear pattern. Further textured interest has been achieved by stitching the cords on soluble fabric enabling decorative non-fraying protrusions to be incorporated.

Machine-embroidered lace (left) *incorporated into paper which is sumptuously coloured with metallic fabric paints. (Judith Ann Peacock)*

Machined cords (right) *were used to construct containers using basketry techniques.* (June Linsley)

This detail of a belt (right) *shows machine-wrapped cords worked in metallic threads which were then plaited, looped or sewn together to make a strong band. Tiny tassels made of machine threads were added for further decoration.*

CORDS

Machine-stitched cords are extremely useful as supporting structures for beads and tassels as well as making straps and attractive edgings. They can also be applied and hand or machined stitched to create an interesting ridged surface. Several cords can be twisted, plaited, spiralled and looped to form intriguing structures. Alternatively a number of cords can be joined together to form a rigid fabric.

To make a cord you will need 'a core' yarn to stitch over. Lengths of knitting wool, string, twine, thin piping cord or fabric rouleaus would all be suitable for this purpose depending on the thickness or rigidity required. Any machine thread can be used to stitch over the centre core but do take note of the wonderful designs, illustrated here, created by the use of multicoloured and metallic threads.

Set your machine for free stitching as described on page 117 and for ease of working remember to fit the wide darning foot (although some of you may prefer to stitch without a foot). Set the machine to zigzag stitch, the width depending on the required cord size. Place the 'core' under the foot, remember to put down the presser foot lever, and, holding both the top and bobbin threads, commence stitching, controlling, steadying and guiding the thread through. Machine backwards and forwards as necessary until it is covered to your satisfaction. For a more textured effect vary the quality of the thread or incorporate short lengths of yarn or fabric fragments.

If several cords need to be joined together to form a band, reset your machine for normal sewing and replace the darning foot with the sewing foot. Reduce the width and length of the zigzag stitch and carefully machine one cord to the next and so on until the required size is achieved. Although more time consuming, cords can also be made using a machine set in this way. To completely cover the 'core', you will have to stitch the length four or five times with a foot which includes a small space beneath to allow the thread to move smoothly and not be flattened. Machine accessories vary depending on the make but darning, hemming, embroidery or cording feet are usually suitable.

This picture (below) *shows the method of placing the 'core' yarn beneath the darning foot and holding it fairly tautly along with the bobbin and top threads. It is then gently guided through to give an even covering of machined zigzag stitches.*

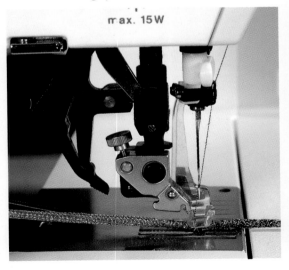

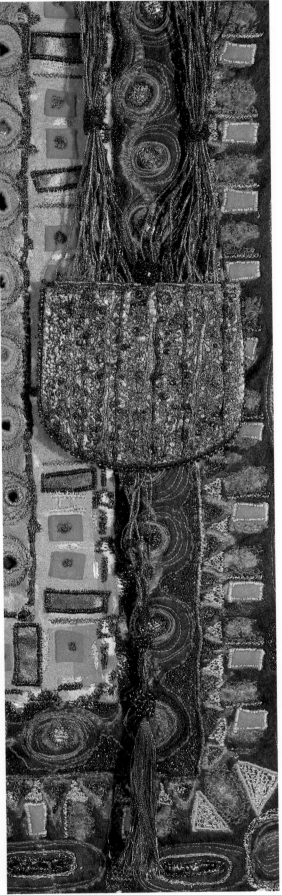

Machined cords (left) *have been used to great effect on this exotic neck purse. Tassels and beads have been incorporated in the straps and finishings. The actual purse shows machine stitches which have encrusted the surface. Worked on a metalized background material, the combination of all these surfaces is most successful. An equally stunning appliqué and machine-stitched panel was used as a background (Eileen Goldschmidt)*

SELECTING A THEME

Having worked through some of the technique exercises, you will hopefully have expanded your basic knowledge about methods of colouring cloth, building up interesting surfaces in fabrics, and about hand and machine embroidery. The next stage is to select a theme which will involve you for some considerable time. New and experienced students, as well as professional artists, seem to grow creatively, developing an individual style and approach to their work when they involve themselves in an in-depth study of a particular subject. The following suggestions may help you to find your own theme to research.

When travelling on a train or in a car consider the sort of view, landmark, object or surface which appeals to you. Is there anything that fascinates you enough for you to steal a second glance? On certain journeys or at particular times of the year, are there sights you deliberately seek out or are drawn to? Perhaps the patchwork pattern of fields, the colour of bluebell-covered woods, a primrose bank or sunlight through trees, fills you with pleasure. Bleak moorlands, ominous clouds or hedgerows full of dog roses and honeysuckle offer different qualities. Are you fascinated by surfaces? Do you collect shells and pebbles or love walking through orchards full of old misshapen apple trees? Are you drawn towards water, babbling brooks, the dark secrets of a rock pool or the rushing of a waterfall? The list is endless.

Themes can be inspired by a book, poetry or by listening to music. They may include aspects which could disturb, please or excite you. Perhaps a recurring theme or a certain quality chosen by the author, poet or composer may well be sympathetic to your views on a particular subject whether it be an abstract theme such as melancholy, happiness, anger or the changing seasons within a landscape. Many of these subjects have fascinated and inspired creative people working in all disciplines.

This painting was coloured with soluble crayons and gouache paint. The centre section shows oilseed rape flowers in full bloom. This interpretation of the rape flowers was created by machining on soluble fabrics. Tiny textural fragments were also made in this way and applied to give a raised surface. Beads were used to give interest.

These delightful houses (opposite page) decorated with 'iron lace' can be found in the Paddington district of Sydney, Australia. Ink and bleach drawings, masking fluid, paper resist and transfer paints have all been used to try out design ideas. Machine-stitched patterns on soluble fabric were inspired by the intricate ironwork. Make a number of small sample pieces before starting a major project.

Free cross stitches (below) have been worked in a variety of directions to create this view of coloured grasses. This sample could act as a trial run before embarking on a larger work.

COLLECTING REFERENCES

If the scope of your theme is too broad your study will tend to be superficial and fragmented. Even abstract imagery succeeds more readily if based on personal experience, observation and information. Choose a theme that you can readily research preferably at first hand. A remote place, a particular item, museum or custom that intrigued you for a fleeting moment should only be explored further if you are confident the information you need is accessible.

You may have selected to observe a view or a tiny section of your garden, a park, field or a hedgerow. The chosen area should be close to, or part of, your everyday environment so that you can study it throughout the year. Changing seasons, varying weather conditions or morning and evening light will give you a wealth of ideas for your projects. Photograph, sketch, make diagrams and take notes on the range of surfaces, possible colour schemes, shapes and views through, as well as noting the general atmosphere, all of which could give you stimulating design sources. Take smaller sections out of context and you will be surprised how your powers of observation will improve with the daily discipline of looking, as will your sketching and note-taking skills.

Even the simplest notes can summon up a visual image, for instance, useful information can be collected while travelling on a train or in a car when there is no time to draw or photograph. To illustrate this point the following

notes on grasses were jotted down on a local train journey on one Autumn day.

'Shiny, glistening, lush round tufts . . .
grasses mixed with Old Man's Beard – straight lines contrasting with pale, curly seedheads . . .
blue grasses – almost turquoise . . .
wet, rotting grasses draped and festooned over the embankment . . .
uprooted, windswept grassy debris, pasted and plastered into the hedgerows . . .
at a distance, in late afternoon light – the bleached, blond grass looks very pink . . .
green, peppered with short tawny tufts . . .
greeny honey-coloured – sun shining brightly on the diagonal leaning stems – like tiny silver strokes.'

Each observation could be the starting point for creating an interesting stitched surface.

MAKING A DESIGN PLAN

Having chosen your theme spend time thinking about it from all aspects. Your collection of sketches, photographs, descriptions and notes could lead you down a number of creative avenues. Systematically work through a number of starting points. You will find that *Book I – Design to Embroider* suggests many approaches to working with a range of media. The following ideas may provide a structure for your work plan:

1. Consider taking shapes and patterns out of context by:
• assembling them into new arrangements such as squares, stripes, diagonals and grids
• repeating and linking the selected units allowing the new patterns which emerge from the background shapes to feature more prominently.
2. Selecting an appropriate technique for your design by:
• studying the characteristics of both the subject matter and the quality of its surface in order to select suitable fabrics and threads
• making trial samples of the same design in a variety of ways.
3. Colour is another strong element within the design process as:
• inspiration for unusual colour schemes where the proportions of colour one to another should be noted
• a way of creating the mood of the piece such as light and sunny, or brooding and menacing
• a method of linking and integrating shapes within a composition.
4. Planning the position of shapes within a

Field images (right) *were printed onto polycotton with transfer paints. The first interpretation was worked in free cross stitches using a variety of threads; the second shows the surface built up in free machine stitching further embellished with hand-stitched french knots.*

This mount (below) *illustrates how assembling photocopies in a variety of arrangements can be most inspirational. The square designs could be interpreted as designs for cushions or quilts. The stitched sample was hand stitched with french knots and eyelets with machine stitching on top.*

piece of work is another important factor to consider. Some of the following suggestions apply when designing embroidery to decorate functional items but more so for wall panels and hangings. Consider:

- varying the viewpoints
- the position of focal points – leading the eye into and around the picture
- designing within a given shape and carefully planning background shapes
- the scale of the design as well as its possible variations within one piece
- the methods of finishing the edges of the project early in the design process.

SHAPES AND PATTERNS OUT OF CONTEXT

As you have already seen in the early part of this book photocopying your drawings and photographs can be a terrific designing aid. As well as saving time, the wealth of composition variations can help you to think laterally and develop your ideas along new avenues. The black and white copies are cheap to make and now that the enlarging and reducing facilities are more readily available you can experiment with changing the scale of all or part of your patterns. This of course depends on which section you wish to focus on or accentuate. For very special projects, design exercises carried out with colour photocopies of your drawings could be most inspiring. However these machines, although becoming more widespread, are still expensive to use.

All the theme subjects illustrated in this section show how design variations can be developed using this technique.

Simplifying shapes and discovering patterns could be a worthwhile path to follow. On studying a drawing or photograph identify some of the main shapes. The embroideries on this page were inspired by the accompanying photograph. You will notice that the lighter areas of flowers and the darker stems suggest a pattern of stripes. These simplified images can often be more clearly shown by taking a black and white photocopy of your colour print which obviously eliminates the colour and in some instances the extraneous detail. It can also exaggerate certain elements and indicate or suggest areas of marks which could be interpreted using stitches of a similar character.

You will notice variations on squares, borders within borders, horizontal and vertical stripes and grids have been illustrated here. The permutations are endless.

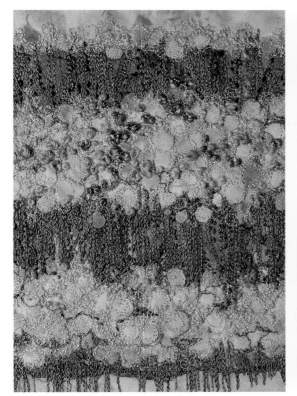

Silk fabric paints were used to colour the silk and cotton ground fabric (above left) *and other fragments of assorted cloth were bonded on top. Free machine embroidery was then added to suggest areas of flowers and stems. French knots, detached chain stitch and seeding give further interest.*

This centre section of a quilted cushion (above right) *was back stitched in medium weight silk threads. Freely applied gold gutta and silk paint was used to colour the background material.*

Oilseed rape field (left). *Painted with coloured inks, the stems in the foreground have been depicted by partially bleaching the ink away. Painted papers including tissue paper have been glued on top for textural effect.*

INTERPRETING A SURFACE

Before interpreting a pattern, surface or view, study them in depth and identify their particular qualities or characteristics. This will enable you to make the appropriate choice of technique, fabric and stitches for your project.

Look carefully at the photographs and sketches on these pages (stitched samples showing the total development of a theme have been deliberately excluded to prevent you forming any preconceived ideas) and consider the following questions.

● Which techniques would be suitable for interpreting these pictures ... piecing and patching, quilting, or machine embroidery?

● If you feel that appliqué would be a suitable method which type would you use? Should the edges of the appliquéd fabric be crisp, softly merging or distressed? How would you stitch the fabric down in an appropriate manner? Would satin-stitched or slip-stitched turned edges, or scatterings of tiny textural stitches be the right choice?

● Some of the pictures show raised areas which could be interpreted in numerous ways. Would you select to work stitches in layers or integrate padded patches or quilted sections?

● Could you identify the main colour schemes and their proportions to one another? Or exaggerate any colour aspects? Would any of these be suitable for quilting or patchwork projects?

● What qualities would you be looking for when selecting fabrics? Consider whether the fabrics should be rough and matt, glistening sheers or soft and velvety.

● Could you exaggerate any of the following features such as the colour, tonal qualities, negative shapes, textures, movement or outlines? Selected tracings would be helpful to develop this train of thought.

● Do any of the pictures provide interesting sections, shapes or motifs which could be taken out of context and repeated as border patterns?

● Could you reassemble, exaggerate, highlight or understate any sections in order to emphasize a particular focal point or colour scheme?

● Could any of your ideas be developed to create a small representative panel, repeating units for a quilt, or a border design to decorate a cushion, garment or an accessory?

Search through your photographs and sketches and apply the same questions. You may discover exciting elements that had not been apparent before. Just one small subject photographed or sketched from varying viewpoints, or light conditions, close to and distanced will provide you with a workable theme for some time.

This collage (above) *coloured with Aquarelle Neocolour was inspired by an old fishing boat in Crete. Layers of peeling paint gave a rich palette of colours as well as an exciting textural surface.*

Intriguing patterned and textured surfaces were found on an old urn (right) *exhibited at the Knossos site in Crete.*

This wonderful picture (opposite page) *was taken from an old Venetian building on Spinalonga in Crete.*

This 'Poppies' image (right) created by a transfer paint monoprint has been used to illustrate the method of placing snippets of thread on the surface to gauge the effect before embarking on the stitchery.

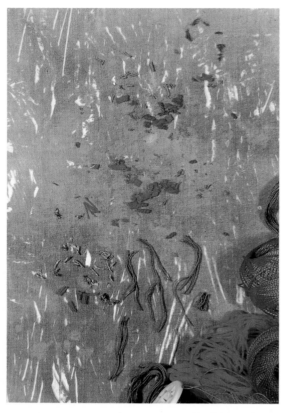

Exquisitely coloured rocks inspired the colour scheme for this log-cabin patchwork quilt (below). Silk and permanent pearl paints were used to colour the cloth. The centre squares show strips of painted silk stitched into canvas. (Elena Pike)

APPROACHES TO COLOUR

Your chosen theme will supply a wealth of information and many ideas for attractive and colourful projects. Wonderful, unusual colour schemes can be extracted and used for abstract patterns for quilts, cushions or fashion embroidery. Methods of selecting and recording the colours and their proportions were illustrated in *The Art of the Needle* (see page 141).

Always be on the lookout for new schemes. The more you look, the more sensitive and aware you will become. Fascinating variations of colour can be revealed when observing the subject in bright or subdued light. In warm countries, rock formations, landscapes and buildings can appear bleached of colour in mid morning whereas the same views, blushed with the early evening sun, can expose rose and tawny hues. The colour of oilseed rape fields also varies tremendously from a breathtaking sunlit lime yellow when backclothed by dark-grey rain clouds to mid tones of golden yellow on a cloudy day. New and fading flowers also show a subtle range of tones.

Some colours are often slightly duller than

you think, containing a wealth of subtle shades. For instance, a field of red poppies can appear startlingly bright but if you actually depicted the tone of red you think it is, it would appear far too dominant within your picture. Red post-boxes or London buses illustrate the same point. If the colour is toned down a shade it will appear more comfortable within its setting. A field of cow parsley or a snow scene also looks very white but if you place a sheet of white paper on a colour print or near an actual flower you will notice that many of the whites are tinged green, grey, yellow, pink and so on. Reflections, cast shadows, distance and light all contribute to make these rich variations.

'White is never white and black is never black' is a helpful remark to remember when designing from natural sources. The effects of placing one colour next to another can lead to many fascinating experiments. There are a number of authoritative books about colour which are worth looking at and will offer you a wealth of information (see page 141).

When looking at an object or a view and attempting to record it visually, half close your eyes. This action will eliminate detail and help you to judge the tone of the colours so they do not appear too dominant within their setting.

The same mistake can be made when selecting threads to work on a particular background. Cut tiny snippets of the proposed colour and place them in the desired position on your embroidery. Stand back, half close your eyes to see if the colour blends in and looks integrated, or does it look (the effect you don't want) 'imposed' on the surface. This approach can save a lot of time and anguish.

A general rule is that however bright or clear you think the colour is, it is usually slightly dirtier and several tones duller or paler than first envisaged. Remember that in most instances 'warm' colour comes to the fore and 'cooler' ones tend to retreat into the background. Always be aware that the softer tones of fabric coloured with fabric paints require a more sensitive selection of threads.

Island Tranquillity (above). *Layers of machine embroidery and fabric pieces were applied to soluble fabric to create a new cloth. Hand stitches have been added in some areas.*

Exciting colour schemes can be found everywhere as can be seen from the wonderful lichen adorning this section of a tree (far left).

This photograph of cow parsley (left) shows the range of off-white tones on display. Compare the white page to the 'whites' in the picture.

VIEWPOINTS

It is always a good idea to consider varying viewpoints and eye levels. Stand back and look at your subject from a distance to see which outline or silhouetted shapes are made against the background. In the coloured sketch and collage of the oilseed rape (page 129), the hedgerows and trees are shown against the skyline whereas the two embroidered examples show lower eye levels. Crouching down to make the initial sketch or photograph resulted in the stitched sample showing a band of flowers featured at the top and not the clouds. An even closer encounter looking through the stems, leaves and flowers would offer an intriguing alternative composition.

Some of the design sketches inspired by Cretan landscapes also show composition variations. The proportions of the blue sky have been much exaggerated compared to the landscape whilst in another version the emphasis has been reversed.

FOCAL POINTS

Deciding on your focal point should feature early in the design plan as your choice of colour, cloth, and technique will enable you to emphasize certain aspects. To illustrate this point the Crete sketches (right) show the same view but at different times of the day. They provided the source for several designs where different focal points had been chosen enlarging and accentuating some areas whilst understating others. To further this aim enticing the viewer to look at your work should be a major challenge. An access point could be placed just within the composition perhaps a line, shape or colour which will subtly take the viewer on a journey into and around the work to a focal point. Take care to have only one as too many will make your project appear 'busy' and disjointed. Linking stitches, drifts of well-placed colour and texture can help unite the composition. Take time to look at the work of some well-known artists. The painter Degas, whether intuitively or by design demonstrates the art of manipulating the viewer's observation. *The Tub*, a pastel drawing and *Two Laundresses*, an oil painting show how the placement of a brush, jug, an arm, the angle of light on a surface all contribute to the piece capturing and retaining the viewer's interest. The same principles can be applied to both figurative and abstract pieces.

The theme 'Cretan landscapes' is very inspirational. This sheet of pictures (right) shows a range of location sketches, designs varying the viewpoints and focal points as well as composition exercises.

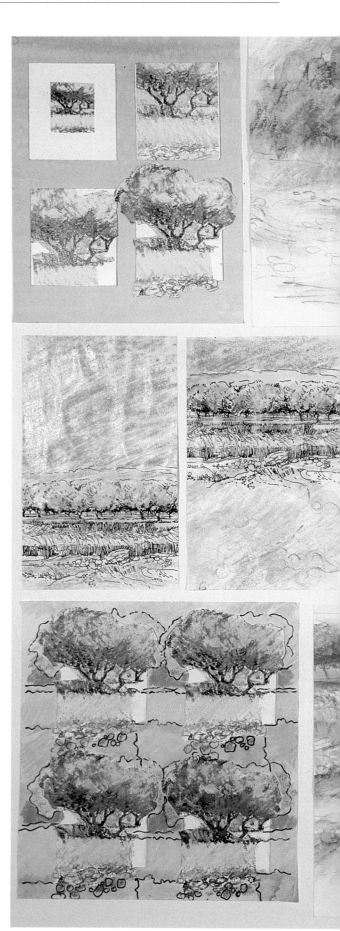

Studies of shells painted in Neocolour II Aquarelle (right). *They provided the design source for the accompanying composition exercises and machine embroidery* (below), *a trial piece for a larger panel.*

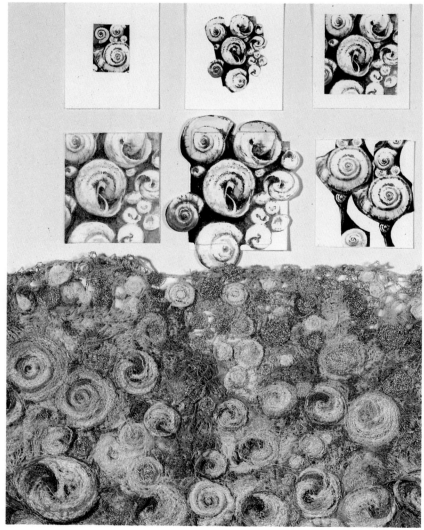

DESIGNS WITHIN SHAPES

Always design or contrive your patterns sympathetically within the given shape to avoid ugly background spaces. This aspect was discussed in detail in *The Art of the Needle* (see page 141).

SCALE

Be aware of possible problems when scaling up your designs to the actual working size. The set of exercises featuring the olive trees on page 135 would most likely transfer to a bigger size quite readily, whereas caution would have to be exercised if the shell ideas on this page were intended to be enlarged. Some of the shapes would be extremely unattractive and clumsy as well as completely losing the delicacy which was the first attraction.

With this in mind, perhaps small units could be assembled into squares with borders to make a large-scale piece. To be on the safe side, always make an outline sketch to scale before embarking on your project (see page 38 in *Book I – Design to Embroider*).

FINISHING AND EDGES

Try and make a decision about the method of finishing the edges of your project at the outset in order for you to select an appropriate technique, type and amount of material and to check its compatibility with the main design source. There are examples to illustrate these points throughout the book.

This set of shell designs (left) *illustrates one way to create less predictable compositions. A small section of the shell drawing was taken out of context and photocopied several times varying the scale from small to large. (A similar exercise was applied to the olive trees on the previous page.) A number of identically sized background papers were cut and selected photocopies placed on them with contrasting effects.*
Top row, from left to right: small section with large border, larger section not retained within a rectangle, large section with narrower surround. Bottom row, from left to right: section taken out of context fitting the background shape, same section showing the shells untrimmed and overlapping the background, a new section taken out of context. The trial sample shows machine-embroidered shells which were worked on soluble fabric to create a new cloth. Single shells were made in the same manner and integrated to develop the textural qualities. Both exercises were inspired by the study of shells (top) *painted in water-soluble crayons.*

PERSONAL THEME

You will have noticed that the island of Crete features prominently throughout both books and in particular this last section. This personal theme has been absorbing, intriguing, surprising and always stimulating. Striving to capture a mood, a particular quality of surface, fleeting changes of light, provide endless opportunities for inspiring stitched works. In general the aim was to create a stitched textile in which the images integrate within their background, enhancing the original view by exploiting the unique qualities of stitchery. This is not always successfully concluded but it is enjoyable and challenging. This total fascination with embroidery has no limits. Therefore it is hoped that you will capture the embroidery 'bug' and enjoy discovering and creating new textile surfaces.

View from the Cove (right). *A compilation of the adjoining drawings inspired this embroidery. The unique background cloth is completely made up of a network of machine stitches initially worked on soluble material.*

Four aspects of a cliff in Crete (below) . *The sketches were painted using water-soluble crayons. Varying light conditions accentuated colour and textured surfaces.*

Abstract Images, using colour, form or texture, which do not necessarily represent recognizable objects.

Acrylic paint A quick drying synthetic paint with a shiny appearance. It is soluble in water and can be used to create textured surfaces.

Airbrush A tool which sprays a fine film of colour onto a surface. Electrical compressors or air-propellant cans provide the supply of pressurized air which projects the colour.

Aquarelle Colouring media such as pencils or crayons which are blendable in water.

Asymmetry Two halves that are not balanced or equal about a central line i.e. they are not mirror images of each other.

Baking parchment Non-stick (silicone) paper used for baking. It seems to be the only paper, apart from the one backing the bonding adhesive, which does not stick to the materials or iron when bonding applied shapes.

Batik Designs made by painting melted wax onto a fabric and dyeing the areas left exposed.

Bonding paper or **transfer fusing web** Paper backed with a fine layer of adhesive. It is used for some types of intricate appliqué as it stiffens the fabric and makes it easier to cut out the shapes.

Buttonhole picots This is worked as small units of detached chain stitch. Work two small straight stitches bringing the thread out just above the left-hand end. Commence working buttonhole stitches over the bar only and not through the fabric. One line produces a ring picot. By turning the needle, and without going into the cloth, make a return journey working buttonhole stitches into the last line of stitches. A number of rows can be worked in this manner resulting in long pieces of stitching which can be manipulated into unusual textural surfaces. Triangular or pointed picots can be made by decreasing one stitch on each journey. To finish off, darn the thread up one side of the picot and fasten off at the back near the original straight stitches.

Cable stitch This machine embroidery stitch gives an interesting textural effect which is achieved by machining on the underside of your work. The resulting raised trailing is most attractive. To indicate where you wish the stitching to go sketch the pattern on the back of your embroidery with an appropriate marker. Remember to place the wrong side of your work uppermost for this particular stitch. Experimentation will illustrate its potential. Fill the bottom bobbin with a thicker thread than usual such as perle or soft crochet cotton. To allow the thread to run through smoothly, you will need to decrease the lower tension. Take care to loosen the screw of the bobbin case on a flat surface so you don't loose it on the floor! The top tension can be left on the normal setting or tightened slightly. Bring the lower thread up through the fabric before commencing. The speed of your machine stitching will determine the textural effect (see page 121).

Card comb A piece of card which has indentations cut out from one end to enable marks to be printed or etched into ink or paint. The size of the card can vary.

Card window A rectangular or square shape cut from a piece of card which can be placed over a design source to identify and select areas of interest. It is very useful when drawing out of context as it cuts out all the distracting peripheral detail.

Cartridge paper Available in several weights, it is suitable for drawing and colour sketches but would need to be stretched for watercolour painting. It is the paper most commonly found in sketchbooks.

Chenille needle A sharp, pointed, short needle with a large eye.

Colourless thickener A colourless 'glue-like' substance which can be added to transfer paints in order to dilute the colour, but not the consistency.

Complementary colour A colour which has the maximum contrast with another and found on opposite sides of the colour wheel i.e. red is the complementary colour of green, blue of orange and yellow of violet.

Conté A hard crayon composed of clay and graphite.

Cotton finish A clear solution applied to the surface of a cotton fabric in order to make the cloth accept transfer-painted prints which are normally intended to be used on synthetic fabrics.

Cretan stitch To work this stitch always keep the thread on the right-hand side of the needle each time a stitch is taken vertically upwards or downwards.

Crewel needle A sharp pointed needle with a long eye.

Disperse dyes An alternative name for transfer paints (see Transfer Paints).

Dressing A substance, sometimes starch or a type of gum, added to fabric in order to stiffen it and to enhance its appearance. It should be thoroughly washed out of any material you intend colouring with fabric paint or dye.

Episcope A machine used to enlarge designs by projecting an image of the drawing against a flat surface. The projected image can be adjusted to the required size making it a very quick and efficient method of enlargement.

Fastening on and off Methods used when commencing and finishing stitching. In most cases begin stitching by fastening on at the back of the fabric by working tiny double stitches, or darning into the cloth or existing stitches. A knot at the end of the thread plus a double stitch is acceptable so long as it does not show through or cobble the right side of the fabric. To fasten off, take your thread through to the back and work a few small stitches as inconspicuously as possible.

Feed dogs These are the 'teeth' on a sewing machine which feed the fabric through the machine under the foot. They are lowered for free machine embroidery so as not to inhibit the movement of the fabric under the needle.

Gesso A paste composed of finely powdered chalk mixed with linseed oil and size or glue. Traditionally used to prime canvases or as a base for the decorative gilding of woodwork. In its solid form it can be carved and, if applied to paper or fabric in fine layers, it creates a flaky textured surface.

Gouache This is an opaque watercolour paint. When dry, lighter colours may be painted over darker shades.

Grid By superimposing a grid over an existing drawing it is possible to enlarge a design. Scale-up the grid to the required size and re-draw the design in the corresponding squares as accurately as possible.

Gum arabic Sap from trees used as a binding medium for water-based paints. When applied to paper and mixed with other media, it cracks to produce textural effects.

Gutta A clear, coloured or metallic fluid used to separate silk paint colours from merging into one another.

Ingres paper A soft, grainy, good quality paper available in subdued colours. It is particularly good to use with pastels and conté crayons.

Insertion stitches or **faggoting** Stitches used to make an open or decorative seam. The edges of fabric with narrow hems are placed opposite each other and tacked (leaving the required space between them) onto a piece of parchment or paper. Various stitches can be worked from one edge to the other without stitching into the paper resulting in a lacy band joining the two fabrics together.

Iridescent colour Colours which shimmer and change to display a spectrum of colour i.e. like those of the rainbow.

Italian quilting A method of quilting where two layers of fabric are stitched together and soft wools or cords inserted between two lines of stitching. The design should therefore be made up of continuous parallel lines.

Ivorex board A fine smooth card which is available in sheets or sketchbooks. It is very robust for working in mixed media.

Linear A design consisting of lines only.

Machine embroidery stitches (see cable, tufting, satin stitch beading and whip stitch.)

Machine lace A term referring to free machine embroidered patterns worked on soluble fabrics.

Masking fluid A fluid which can be painted onto paper to mask certain lines or areas of the design in order to resist watercolour paint which can be applied on top. It can be rubbed away using a finger or putty rubber.

Medium Any suitable material (such as oil, water, wax etc.) with which pigment is mixed to make it usable. In a more general sense it refers to the material from which a piece of work is created, for example acrylics or pastels.

Monochrome A painting or design created from one colour only.

Monoprinting This is the process whereby figurative or abstract patterns are drawn into a layer of printing ink or paint (including fabric paint) which has been rolled on to a smooth surface such as glass or plastic. A print is taken by gently pressing paper or fabric over the image.

Motif A distinctive feature of a design or unit of pattern.

Nib In the context of this book, a nib is a fine metal pointed accessory with a hole in it which is fitted to the nozzle of a pot containing gutta. It controls the flow of the fluid enabling fine lines to be drawn on cloth.

Pattern A unit of design repeated in orderly or random groupings.

Paillette A type of spangle or sequin usually made of plastic and often shaped as flowers, leaves or shells.

Pigments The colouring matter which is mixed with other substances to form media such as paints or pencils. Originally they were derived from natural sources but are now often chemically based.

PVA glue or **Marvin Medium** (equivalent makes in the USA, Sobo Glue and Elmer's Glue). A non-toxic, very good, strong all purpose glue which dries transparent and shiny. It can be diluted with water and mixed with colour to make textured surfaces.

Pipette A plastic dropper which transfers small amounts of liquid (similar to a medical eardropper).

Plate Produced by manufacturers where machine feed dogs do not lower. Made of metal or plastic they can cover the feed dog to make them inoperative. Used for darning or free machining.

Polyester cotton A fabric woven in cotton and polyester (synthetic) yarns.

Polyester viscose A fabric made from polyester (synthetic) threads and viscose (a manmade material derived from vegetable fibres).

Presser foot lever This enables the presser foot to be lowered in order to engage the upper thread tension. Always remember to do this when free machining without a foot in place.

Primary colours Colours which cannot be made by mixing together other colours i.e. red, blue and yellow.

Procion powder A dye powder available from specialist shops. Normally it is used for dyeing fabrics when following the correct recipe containing a fixative. When mixed with cold water it can produce marvellous colours for designing but should be handled carefully with rubber gloves.

Resists Any barrier, such as wax, masking tape or masking fluid, which can be applied to a background and prevents colour from penetrating the covered areas.

Rouleau In the context of this book a rouleau means a fabric strip cut on the bias which has been machined and turned to make a hollow tube. Used for ties and trims on fashion accessories, they can be padded with cord or partially covered with machine stitches.

Ruching A method of gathering strips or pieces of fabric into little folds, frills or indentations.

Satin stitch beading This is a machine embroidery stitch created by selecting the satin stitch programme and machining several stitches on the same spot, lifting the needle and moving the frame before commencing with more satin stitches. Random blocks of straight stitches contrast with the fine thread joining one block to another.

Scrim Open weave fabric of cotton, linen or hessian which can be pulled to make holes. Available in a variety of thicknesses and textures from the very delicate to coarse.

Shadow quilting This is a delicate form of quilting whereby two layers of semi-transparent fabric, such as organdy or voile, are stitched together with coloured fabrics or threads sandwiched between them. The base fabric could be an opaque cloth printed with a coloured image which will show through in a 'shadowy' way once the sheer fabric has been placed on top.

Shot fabrics These are fabrics where the warp is one colour and the weft another which results in a surface that changes in tone according to the play of light.

Slubbed A thread which has been spun with irregular lumps or thick areas.

Soluble fabrics These come in two forms: one is soluble in cold water the other in boiling water. The former is a thin plastic material which you must take care to protect from accidental spillages, sneezing etc. The latter is an 'organdy' type fabric which seems to withstand more layering of machine stitching than the cold water-soluble fabric. It, of course, will only dissolve in boiling water.

Stiletto A sharp pointed tool used for making holes in fabric to ease thicker threads through or for making eyelet holes.

Stylized The adaptation of an image within the constraints of a particular style.

Sugar paper A cheap but strong paper which is available in a limited colour range.

Symmetry A shape in which each half is a mirror image of the other and is balanced about in a central axis.

Tacking or **basting** a long straight stitch.

Texture A quality of surface, for example, rough, smooth or ridged.

Tissue A fine translucent paper. In the context of *Book II – Stitched Images* it means a fine shimmering fabric made from metallic or lurex threads.

Tone The degree of lightness or darkness of a colour.

Transfer fabric paints and crayons or **Disperse dyes** These can be used to create patterns on a smooth paper and when dry ironed onto a suitable fabric.

Tufting A machine embroidery stitch with a loopy texture that can be achieved by fitting a tailor tacking foot and setting the machine onto the zigzag stitch. The width or spacing of the stitch and the choice of thread will give variety. This stitch can be worked with the machine set for either normal or free work. Consider working free running stitches with parts of the design to secure the loops and break up or flatten the loopy surface. Alternatively some of the loops could be cut for a varied effect.

Voided shapes Negative or unworked shapes within a design.

Voiding Small areas left unworked between areas of design to emphasize the shapes.

Watercolour paper A thick, relatively expensive paper which can be made from rags. The very heavy varieties can be as thick as card but have a soft surface which does not buckle when used with watery media.

Whip stitch A machine embroidery stitch worked by tightening the top tension and at the same time loosening the lower one. The top thread can be slightly thicker than the base one, for example, normal sewing thread 50 compared to a finer machine thread 30.

STITCH DIAGRAMS

Buttonhole (a) and
Detached Buttonhole (b)

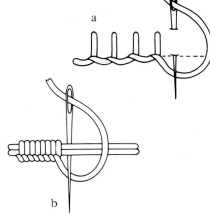

Varieties of chain stitch: detached chain
stitch (a and b), ordinary chain (c), twisted
chain (d and e), raised chain band worked
in a line (f) and freely, as a filling (g),
knotted cable chain (h, i and j) and rosette
chain (k, l and m).

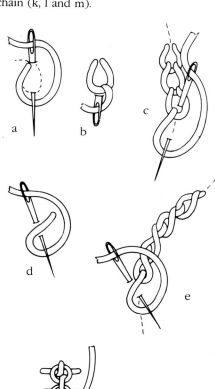

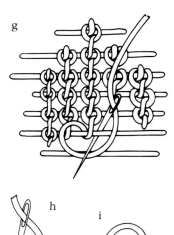

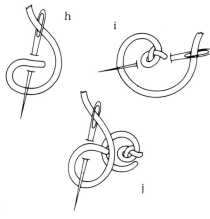

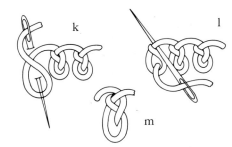

Couching

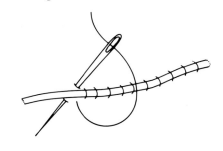

Cross stitch

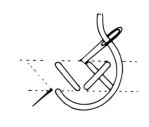

Double Knot Stitch

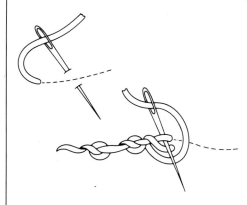

Fly Stitch

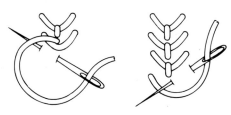

French Knot

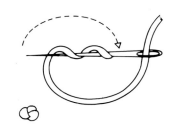

Herringbone Stitch

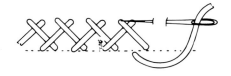

Straight Stitch (a) and
Seeding (b)

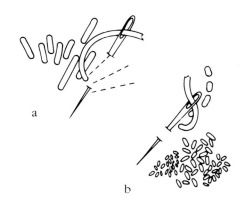

ACKNOWLEDGEMENTS

We would like to thank the following people for their enthusiastic help and support throughout the making of these books: especially to our husbands, Philip Littlejohn and Steve Udall for their continued encouragement, their help with photography and with some of the text; to our children, Hannah Littlejohn for her valued contributions, to Victoria Udall for typing Book II and for helping with the index, and to Nick Udall for reference photography; to Zarina Bastani for additional typing; to our friends the professional artists Julia and Alex Caprara, Claire Johnson and Audrey Walker for generously allowing us to include their work; to Valerie Buckingham, Senior Editor at Century, to Cindy Richards, our Editor and Sue Storey our Designer for being such a super and happy team to work with; to Patrick McLeavey for the care he took over his photographic contributions; to Janet Wilcox; to all our students for their hard work, loyalty and commitment, and for allowing us to use their work; and finally to our special friend and terrific photographer Dudley Moss.

READING LIST

GENERAL
The Art of the Needle
by Jan Beaney
Century, London, 1988

Fabrics for Embroidery
by Jean Littlejohn
B. T. Batsford Ltd., London, 1986
David & Charles Inc., Vermont, 1986

Needlework School
by The Embroiderers' Guild Practical Study Group
Windward, London, 1984

STITCHES
Stitches: New Approaches
by Jan Beaney
B. T. Batsford Ltd., London, 1985
David & Charles Inc., Vermont, 1985

Mary Thomas's Dictionary of Embroidery Stitches: New Edition
by Jan Eaton
Hodder & Stoughton, London, 1983

Embroidery Stitches
by Barbara Snook
B.T. Batsford Ltd., London, 1963

100 Embroidery Stitches
J. & P. Coats Ltd., Glasgow, 1989

MACHINE EMBROIDERY
Machine Embroidery
by Gail Harker
Merehurst, London, 1990

Machine Embroidery: Stitch Techniques
by Valerie Campbell-Harding and Pamela Watts
B. T. Batsford Ltd., London, 1989

Machine Embroidery: Lace and See-through Techniques
by Moyra McNeill
B. T. Batsford Ltd., London, 1985
David & Charles Inc., Vermont, 1985

FABRIC PAINTS
Fabric Painting for Embroidery
by Valerie Campbell-Harding
B.T. Batsford Ltd., London, 1991

DESIGN AND MATERIALS
How to Make your own Recycled Paper
by Malcolm Valentine and Rosalind Dace
British Wildlife Promotions Ltd., Search Press, Tunbridge Wells, 1990

Felt Making
by Inge Evers
A. & C. Black Ltd., London, 1981

Paper Pleasures
by Faith Shannon
Mitchell Beazley, London, 1989

Drawing and Design for Embroidery
by Richard Box
B. T. Batsford Ltd., London, 1988
David & Charles Inc., Vermont, 1988

Drawing: a Practical Step-by-Step Guide
A Mitchell Beazley Handbook
Mitchell Beazley, London, 1982

Embroidery and Colour
by Constance Howard
B. T. Batsford Ltd., London, 1976
Van Nostrand Reinhold Co., New York, 1976

The Elements of Colour
by Johannes Itten
Van Nostrand Reinhold Co., New York and London, 1983

The Textile Design Book
by Karin Jerstorp
A. & C. Black Ltd., London, 1989

The Art and Craft of Papier-Mâché
by Juliet Bawden
Mitchell-Beazley, London, 1989

INSPIRATIONAL
Embroidered Textiles: Traditional Patterns from Five Continents
by Sheila Paine
Thames & Hudson, London, 1990

Africa Adorned
by Angela Fisher
Collins Harvill, London, 1984

The Grammar of Ornament
by Owen Jones
Studio Editions, London, 1988

MAGAZINES AND VIDEOS ON EMBROIDERY

The following publications include up-to-date information about exhibitions, workshops, courses and suppliers.

UNITED KINGDOM
Crafts
published six times a year by:
The Crafts Council
8 Waterloo Place, London SW1 4AT

Embroidery
published quarterly by:
The Embroiderers' Guild
Apartment 41, Hampton Court Palace
East Molesey, Surrey KT8 9AU
(Details on membership of the Guild, which is open to anyone, can also be obtained from this address.)

UNITED STATES
Fiberarts
published six times a year by:
Nine Press
50 College Street
Asheville, NC 28801

The Flying Needle
published quarterly by:
The National Standards Council of American Embroiderers
588 St. Charles Ave,
NE, Atlanta, GA 30308

Needle Arts
published quarterly for its members by:
The Embroiderers' Guild of America
200 Fourth Avenue
Louisville, KY 40202
(Membership of the Guild is open to anyone; for details, apply to the above address.)

Stitch Images
presented by Jan Beaney and featuring Jean Littlejohn. Available from:
Stitch Images
PO Box 7, Dursley,
Gloucester, GL11 5TW

STOCKISTS AND SUPPLIERS

The following addresses may be of use to British readers.

Barnyarns
Old Pitts Farm
Langrish
Petersfield
Hampshire GU32 1RG
(general embroidery supplies, fabric paints)

Bernina
Bogod House
50-52 Great Sutton Street
London EC1V 0DJ
(sewing machines)

Borovicks Fabrics Ltd.
16 Berwick Street
London W1V 4HP
(exotic, sheer, shot and novelty fabrics)

Candle Makers Supplies
28 Blythe Road
London W14 0HA
(dyes, fabrics paints, fabrics)

Coats Patons Crafts Ltd
McMullen Road
Darlington
County Durham DL1 1YQ
(full range of Anchor embroidery threads, information and lists of stockists)

L. Cornellison & Son Ltd.
105 Great Russell Street
London WC1B 3RY
(art supplies, metallic powders, iridescent crayons and gouache)

DMC Creative World
Pullman Road
Wigston
Leicester LE8 2DY
(DMC threads, information and lists of stockists)

Madeira (UK) Ltd.
Thirsk Industrial Park
York Road
Thirsk
North Yorkshire YO7 3BX
(manufacturers of machine threads, cold and boiling water-soluble fabrics; information and lists of stockists)

Pfaff
Pfaff House
East Street
Leeds LS9 8EH
(sewing machines)

Shades at Mace and Nairn
89 Crane Street
Salisbury
Wiltshire SP1 2PY
(Deka and Pebeo fabric paints and general embroidery supplies)

George Weil
Showroom
18 Hanson Street
London W1P 7DB

Mail order
Reading Arch Road
Redhill
Surrey RH1 1H6
(Dyes, fabric paints and fabrics)

Whaleys (Bradford Ltd.)
Harris Court
Great Horton
Bradford
West Yorkshire BD7 4EQ
(range of fabrics prepared for dyeing, including silk cotton and felt, cold and boiling water-soluble fabrics; minimum length requirement)

USA STOCKISTS AND SUPPLIERS

Please write to the companies below for purchasing and most other information

Pebeo of America Inc.
PO Box 373
Willeston
Vermont 05495

Susan Bates Inc.
212 Middlesex Avenue
Chester
Connecticut 06412
(distributor for Anchor embroidery threads)

DMC Corporation
Port Kearny Building # 10
South Kearny
New Jersey 07032-0650
(DMC threads, information and lists of stockists)

Madeira (USA) Ltd
PO Box 6068
30 Bayside Court
Laconia
New Hampshire
03246
(manufacturer of cotton, metallic and synthetic yarns, boiling and cold water-soluble fabrics)

Pelikan Inc.
200 Beasley Drive
Franklin
Tennessee 37064-3998

Decart Inc.
PO Box 309
Morrisville
Vermont 05661
(suppliers of Deka products)

INDEX

Page references in *italics* denote illustrations and captions.